THE BELIEFNET GUIDE TO

*I*SLAM

Also Available

THE BELIEFNET GUIDE TO *K*ABBALAH

THE BELIEFNET GUIDE TO *E*VANGELICAL *C*HRISTIANITY

THE BELIEFNET GUIDE TO *G*NOSTICISM AND
*O*THER *V*ANISHED *C*HRISTIANITIES

THE BELIEFNET GUIDE TO

*I*SLAM

Hesham A. Hassaballa
and
Kabir Helminski

Three Leaves Press

Doubleday / New York

THREE
LEAVES
PRESS

PUBLISHED BY DOUBLEDAY
a division of Random House, Inc.

THREE LEAVES PRESS and its colophon are trademarks of
Random House, Inc., and DOUBLEDAY and its colophon are
registered trademarks of Random House, Inc.

Library of Congress Cataloging-in-Publication Data
Hassaballa, Hesham A.
    The Beliefnet guide to Islam / Hesham A. Hassaballa
and Kabir Helminski.
        p.   cm.
    Includes bibliographical references.
    1. Islam. 2. Islam—Doctrines. I. Title: Guide to Islam.
II. Helminski, Kabir Edmund 1947– III. Title.

BP161.3.H365 2006
297—dc22

                                        2005052855

ISBN 0-385-51454-9
PRINTED IN THE UNITED STATES OF AMERICA

First Three Leaves Press Edition

10 9 8 7 6 5 4 3 2 1

CONTENTS

September 11, 2001, seemed to confirm that the world was in the midst of a clash of civilizations. After all, the nineteen hijackers who took command of civilian planes and crashed them into buildings in New York and Washington were from a different part of the world, and adhered to a religion, Islam, that most Americans only dimly understood. This was an undeclared state of war. Commentators looked around for an explanation and found a ready-made theory: Samuel Huntington of Harvard University had already written a book entitled *The Clash of Civilizations,* in which he predicted that the West, led by the United States, would end up in an ultimate confrontation with other civilizations, especially the Muslim world. Huntington had been inspired by Bernard Lewis of Princeton University, who had argued for years that the Muslim world's failure to compete with the West had given birth to hostility, even rage, that was about to explode. In the weeks and months following September 11, it appeared that these two men's theories were, terrifyingly, coming true.

But in the midst of those terrible days, hopeful signs appeared. Men and women of good faith reached out, hoping to create a dialogue between these civilizations. There were unlikely partners in the endeavor. President Mohammed Khatami of Iran actually talked of a "dialogue of civilizations" in the United Nations. Jonathan Sacks, the Chief Rabbi of the United Kingdom, wrote an excellent book embodying the essence of dialogue at the heart of the Abrahamic faiths—*The Dignity of Difference* (2003). Lord George Carey, former archbishop of Canterbury, along with James Wolfensohm, former president of the World Bank, created "The World Faiths Development Dialogue," which argues that in order to tackle economic poverty we need to look at the spiritual context in which we live. Shortly after September 11, Oprah Winfrey hosted a program entitled "Islam 101." And Bruce Lustig, senior rabbi of the Washington-Hebrew Congregation, hosted the first annual Abrahamic Summit there in 2002, which continues to this day—now at the National Cathedral. Professor Judea Pearl— the father of Danny Pearl, who was murdered in Karachi—and I have begun together to promote Jewish-Muslim understanding. These were attempts by brave individuals to stand against the tidal wave of emotions unleashed by the simplistic, but powerful, idea of the clash of civilizations.

These days, the Muslim world is still everywhere in the news. American troops are on the ground in Iraq and Afghanistan and involved in exchanging fire with Muslims. The constant stories of prisoner abuse from U.S. prison camps continues to anger and agitate Muslims. There can be nothing more urgent than understanding Islam. As a scholar of Islam— and as a Muslim myself—I believe it is imperative that Muslims come forward to begin the process of understanding and bridge-building. This book is one such attempt.

There are many excellent scholarly books on Islam that have

been published recently. Tamara Sonn's *A Brief History of Islam* (2004) takes us through the early days of Islam, the time of its golden age and its great empires, the colonial era when Muslim lands were subjected to European colonization, and finally the current situation. Seyyed Hossein Nasr takes a more spiritual look at Islam, pointing out its harmony with Jewish and Christian values as well as its contribution to a peaceful global future, in his book *The Heart of Islam: Enduring Values for Humanity* (2004). I, too, have written books on the subject. *Islam Today: A Short Introduction to the Muslim World* is an overview, which presents Islam's history, culture, society, and main features. *Discovering Islam: Making Sense of Muslim History and Society* (1988), became the basis for a six-part BBC television series entitled *Living Islam*. A more recent book, *Islam Under Siege: Living Dangerously in a Post-Honor World* (2003), examines Muslim societies closely and argues that there is transformation and change taking place, which in turn affects Western societies.

The Beliefnet Guide to Islam, while not a work of scholarship, is a much-needed contribution to the public understanding of Islam. The authors give us an insightful look at the religion, painstakingly laying out the essentials of the faith: the need to study Islam as a religion; a discussion of Muhammad, the messenger of God; and a fascinating look at the Qur'an, the message of Muhammad. Indeed, the authors are right to link the messenger and the message. Together the two provide the Shariah, or "the path," for Muslims. Muslims, no matter where they live or what nationality they are, need to be constantly engaged in understanding the Shariah in order to live up to and interpret the faith.

The Beliefnet Guide to Islam also tells us about the Five Pillars of Islam—faith in one God and the Prophet as his final messenger, prayer, charity, fasting, and pilgrimage. We learn the meaning of *jihad*, misunderstood in the West as a term for "religious war." The book provides us a detailed chronology tracing the development of Islam from the time of the Prophet to the spread of Islam, and brings it up to date. The book also discusses the role of women—one of the most explosive issues among Muslims and their critics. The authors ask the question: What are the primary sources of the Islamic faith (namely the Qur'an and hadith) that would justify sexism, patriarchy, or the devaluation of women? "There are serious issues to be confronted, and we are living through a time of re-evaluation, reinterpretation, and reconciliation," they write. By carefully deconstructing Islam's sacred texts, they show that the Qur'an shows women in a positive light and grants equal rights to women. And they point out that on the basis of the Qur'an, the struggle for women's rights in Islamic societies is going forward.

The authors' love for their religion comes shining through when they discuss the Prophet of Islam. They point out that for Muslims it is important to add the words "peace be upon him" as a special blessing when talking about the extraordinary prophets from God. This blessing is particularly used when mentioning the Prophet. However, the authors are aware that they are writing for an American audience; use of these words may clutter up the text, so they leave them out. Does this mean their love and respect for the Prophet is diminished?

Not at all. In personal sidebars, Dr. Hassaballa describes his love for the Prophet—his visit to Muhammad's tomb in Medina when he performed the long-awaited pilgrimage—the Hajj—required of all Muslims once in a lifetime. He describes his attempts to push through the large crowds of worshippers to get as near as possible to the actual tomb. He cannot contain his emotions. He has tears in his eyes because he is there "to see my beloved."

This description itself should tell us a great deal about how Islam is interpreted in our world. To Muslims, the Prophet of Islam is a figure of compassion and mercy, capable of evoking tears of love in the eyes of a physician from Chicago. Yet in America, public religious figures have publicly called our Prophet a "terrorist" and a "demon-possessed pedophile." Perhaps you can imagine how deeply hurt Muslims feel when they hear these cruel descriptions of the figure that inspires in us so much love and compassion.

Muslims have also suffered through the Qur'an controversy, in which *Newsweek* reported that copies of the Qur'an had been flushed down toilets at Guantanamo Bay in an attempt to humiliate prisoners there. *Newsweek* retracted the story, although there remain conflicting reports about whether it may be true, at least in part. What Americans did not fully realize was the offense and outrage among Muslims regarding the story about the desecration of the Qur'an. Muslims believe the Qur'an is the word of God and therefore must be respected. In their reverence for the Qur'an as the embodiment of the divine message, the nearest equivalent would be the figure of Jesus for Christians. That is why passions were so high when the *Newsweek* story broke. Some twenty people lost their lives in the protests in Afghanistan.

The verbal assaults on the Prophet, and the *Newsweek* allegations, were broadcast extensively in the Muslim world and fed into anger and violence against America. This anger helped recruit more militant Islamists to attack and harm Americans

or the interests of America. Unfortunately, the story about the
desecration of the Qur'an is not over, and it continues to create
resentment against Americans.

It's important to underline the cause-and-effect connection:
the greater the attacks on the Prophet and the Qur'an, the
more the sense of alienation among Muslims. For these attacks
are seen throughout the Muslim world as an attack on Islam itself, negating American attempts to win the hearts and minds
of the Muslim world. So while the United States sets out
to win friends in the Muslim world, some Americans have
harmed that effort by attacking important parts of our religion
and thereby alienating millions of Muslims in the process. This
book goes a long way in helping to explain the connection.

Why should non-Muslims want to read a book on Islam?
First, because understanding Islam is no longer a luxury left to
the scholar. Until recently the United States was recognized
as a Judeo-Christian nation. Now we realize it is a Judeo-
Christian-Islamic nation. Muslims derive their religion from
the Judeo-Christian tradition. Their notion of God, the
prophets, the messengers, the holy text, an afterlife, and the
core values organizing Judeo-Christian societies are similar.
Abraham is a common patriarch and prophet to all three faiths.
There are, of course, theological differences, but the similarities
far outweigh the differences. Though demographers quibble
over the numbers, most agree that between 2 million and 7
million Muslims live in the United States—a population as
large as the Jewish population, and perhaps even larger. The
next generation of Muslims will hold public office, appear in
media, and hold important academic and business posts. Even
today, one of the great icons of American culture is a Muslim:
Muhammad Ali, the boxer.

Second, America is fighting a "war on terror" involving Muslims—Osama bin Laden and other leaders of Al Qaeda chief among them. Yet some of America's closest allies are also Muslim, because the "war on terror" cannot be fought without a close relationship with President Pervez Musharraf of Pakistan, President Hamid Karzai of Afghanistan, and acting Prime Minister Ibrahim al-Jaafari of Iraq. Musharraf has captured and killed more people in this connection than any other ally. Little wonder that the United States promoted Pakistan to the status of "major non-NATO ally." Therefore, for America to understand those it is dealing with—both foes and friends—it needs to understand their religion: Islam.

Islam is now a global religion of about 1.3 billion people, and it is growing. Scholars say it is one of the few world civilizations that will continue to grow rapidly in the twenty-first century. The Muslim world now includes about fifty-seven states, one of which (Pakistan) is nuclear. And there are other Muslim nations (such as Iran) with nuclear ambitions.

There is another reason to understand Islam. In their book *The Pivotal States: A New Framework for U.S. Policy in the Developing World*, Robert Chase, Emily Hill, and Paul Kennedy posit that there are nine important nations on which American foreign policy in the immediate future will rest: Algeria, Brazil, Egypt, India, Indonesia, Mexico, Pakistan, South Africa, and Turkey. Five of them—Algeria, Egypt, Indonesia, Pakistan, and Turkey—are Muslim. If five of the nations on which America bases its foreign policy are Muslim, surely it is important to have a good understanding of this religion and its history and culture.

To put it mildly, this is an interesting time for relations between the United States and the Muslim world. Books are being published on an unprecedented scale. Some authors argue that Muslims should be tortured in interrogation or should be interned, as Japanese-Americans were during World War II. They seem unaware of the irony of advocating torture and detention in a nation that has prided itself on human rights, civil liberties, and cultivation of individual freedom. These authors seem unaware that they are chipping away at one of the freest and most democratic societies in history. Their dislike of Islam, it seems, overrides their regard for great American virtures.

This constant barrage of negative association around Islam has hardened public opinion against Muslims. Crosses have been burned outside mosques. Muslim girls wearing the *hijab* have been attacked. Muslim men have been set upon; even followers of Sikhism, because they wore turbans and beards, were assaulted and in some cases killed because people thought they were Muslim. There is little doubt that Muslims are scrutinized and harassed by authorities compared to other groups when they are traveling. And when Muslims are subjected to gross human rights violations, when their religion is attacked in the media, or when they themselves are physically assaulted, few Americans are prepared to express outrage.

In order for us to build bridges between America and the Muslim world, we need to identify those issues Muslims are most sensitive about. Within the United States, Muslims are most uneasy about the Patriot Act. They complain about racial profiling and believe they are being unfairly targeted simply because of their religion. On the international stage, most Muslims are unhappy about the continuing violence in Iraq. The death and destruction only seem to increase. That is why when the Qur'an incident took place it fed into an already existing unease felt by Muslims about U.S. relations with the Muslim world. On the other hand, Muslims have always appreciated the attempts by American leaders to reach out and have responded positively to the Abrahamic dialogue that has begun across the land.

When two civilizations look at each other through the filter of hostility and ignorance, it is easy to worry that they are heading for a global confrontation, and violence is one consequence. It is imperative to begin the process of understanding and dialogue, which cannot take place without some idea of the religion of Islam. It is therefore with gratitude that readers should pick up *The Beliefnet Guide to Islam*. I express my gratitude for a book that provides another opportunity for understanding my religion and culture.

INTRODUCTION

Recent events have generated an intense interest in the religion known as Islam. The attacks of September 11, 2001, the ongoing brutal conflicts in the Middle East and Asia, and the purported threat of an international terrorist organization known as Al Qaeda are leading many people to ask questions about Islam's beliefs, practices, and goals. Outside the Muslim world many may be wondering whether Islam is a "religion of peace," as has been asserted, or whether we are facing a true clash of civilizations. How could religion motivate nineteen young Muslim men to hijack four planes and attack the World Trade Center and the Pentagon? What cause drives these suicide bombers to sacrifice both their own lives and those of innocent civilians? Why are women in some Muslim countries shrouded in black cloth and supposedly oppressed? Why are the Arab countries so far behind the rest of the world in major criteria of scientific development and human freedom?

On the other hand, history reveals that Islam has made a vast contribution to human life. While Europe was in its Dark Ages, Islamic civilization was the most advanced in the world. For centuries it supported a relatively enlightened, tolerant, multicultural civilization. It gave birth to the first universities, supported extensive libraries and hospitals that were free to all, and sustained a system of business ethics that encouraged world trade. Furthermore, religious minorities were generally protected, as evidenced, for instance, by the continuity of Christian and Jewish culture over thirteen centuries in Jerusalem. During the Middle Ages, Islamic Spain was far ahead of the rest of Europe, and the three Abrahamic faiths flourished there in harmony. Judaism even reached a golden age under Islamic rule in Spain. For many centuries Islamic civilization embraced science; Muslim scholars revived, preserved, and advanced the scientific and medical knowledge of the Greeks when it was lost to the rest of the world. Islam even influenced and transformed Christian theology through Thomas Aquinas and others who were deeply influenced by Muslim commentators on the Greek classics. Any serious student of history must conclude that Islam has been a major civilizing influence in world affairs.

Yet troubling questions are also arising today for Muslims themselves. Questions such as: Why, if we possess a revelation from God and such a noble history, are we in the state we're in? From personal observation we can say that while some Muslims are playing the blame game, shifting responsibility to colonialism, Zionist conspiracies, and American imperialism, many more are sincerely asking important and difficult questions of themselves.

For a long time much of the world was comfortable in its ignorance of one-fifth of the world's population, but that complacency has been shattered. Islam is demanding attention. This book will try to answer some of the basic questions about Islam from a layperson's point of view. It will try to give a sense of what it is like to live within the spiritual universe of Islam. This is neither an apology for nor a critique of contemporary Islam. Our hope is that we can increase the understanding of Islamic values and motivations, so that you can judge for yourself whether there is an essential conflict between Islam and the West or an opportunity for cooperation.

It is urgent that we address the kinds of fears that non-Muslims have about Islam. There is a struggle for the soul of Islam going on. Needless to say, Islam is not a monolithic community of belief. But it may be possible, by referring to the primary sources, especially the Qur'an, to ask whether Islam is inherently supportive of human rights, liberal values, and religious pluralism. Some of the questions that should be addressed include:

What is Islam's relationship to other faiths? Does Islam tolerate other religions when it comes to power? Is there a basis for religious pluralism under Islamic orthodoxy?

Does Islam recognize freedom of conscience, thought, expression, and dissent? What are the limits on freedom of religion?

Does Islam condone the use of force in achieving political goals?

What is meant by the term kafir *(usually translated as "infidel" or "unbeliever")?*

Does the Qur'an ever condone the killing of kafirs*?*

What is the Qur'anic teaching on the position of women? Are they to be under the domination of men? Do they have fewer rights than men?

Does Islam have an agenda to dominate the world? Can Islam coexist with secular democracy?

Furthermore, Islam might offer a unique point of view on some of the human crises we face today:

How can Islam shed light on the ecological crisis? Is there a clear rationale for Islamic environmentalism?

How can Islam shed light on the economics of globalization and the unrestrained power of capital? Or is Islamic economics, which supposedly forbids charging interest, an anachronistic and impractical system?

What is the place of altruism in Islam? What are some examples of those principles that oppose the commercialism of contemporary consumer society?

What would be an Islamic perspective on just war and on the weapons industry that is consuming so much of the world's talent and resources?

Are Muslims willing to put their knowledge and beliefs into the service of humanity, joining other groups that are working for the same goals? In other words, can they begin to demonstrate that Islam serves humanity, not just the apparent interests of those who are nominally Muslims?

Reflecting on these questions might begin to reveal a more nuanced understanding of the broad range of Islamic thought and to shift perceptions from the simplistic, fear-based stereotypes of Islam that are common in our media and public discourse.

A NOTE ON QUR'ANIC TRANSLATION
AND OTHER LANGUAGE MATTERS

The translations of the Qur'anic text will sometimes be our own but are generally based closely on that of Muhammad Asad, and occasionally on the Thomas Cleary translation. Muhammad Asad was a Jewish convert to Islam who became one of the foremost Muslim intellectuals of the twentieth century. Thomas Cleary is a scholar of Eastern languages and civilizations, and he has recently issued a new translation of the Qur'an in contemporary English. Many translations of the Qur'an are replete with parenthetical phrases, usually signifying that the translator has supplied a word or two believed to be part of the meaning but not literally present in the Arabic. For the sake of readability we have reduced the number of such parenthetical comments, either eliminating them altogether or incorporating them into the translation when we believe their meanings are intrinsic to the Arabic.

The name for the Creator we will use is "God," even though Muslims call the Creator "Allah." For the purposes of this book, the terms are interchangeable, because there is not a "Muslim God" apart from that of other religions. The Qur'an clearly proposes that one God has sent countless prophets to inspire all human communities in all times, even if we human beings often corrupt the essential message through our own egoism.

We have limited the use of the customary Islamic phrase "Peace be upon him" from after the names of the prophets that are cited in the text. This is for the sake of our largely non-Muslim readership, but it is not intended to lessen the respect accorded to God's prophets. May God's peace, blessings, and mercy be upon them all.

1

WHAT IS THIS RELIGION CALLED ISLAM?

The religion we know as Islam began in Arabia in the sixth century when a man named Muhammad began to experience a series of "revelations," or communications from the Divine. He was a reluctant prophet at first, even fearing that his own sanity was in question, but his beloved wife, Khadija, said, "Muhammad, a man like you doesn't go crazy." Over a period of twenty-three years he would receive periodic guidance from this Divine Source, often in response to the particular needs of his growing community, in a language of great depth and beauty. This revelation is called the Qur'an and it is the foremost inspiration, reference point, and final authority of the religion of Islam. Here is some of what it says about itself:

> God has sent down the best of teaching in a Book fully harmonious with itself, repeating the truth in manifold ways and often repeated in recitation; A Book that causes the skins of all who stand in awe of their Lord to shiver, but in the end their skins and their hearts soften at the remembrance of God. Such is God's guidance. (39:23)

And We have sent down to you, step by step, this Book,
to make all matters clear, and as guidance and grace and
good tidings unto all who have submitted themselves to
God. God commands justice, the doing of good, and giving to one's relatives; and He forbids all that is shameful
and runs counter to reason, in addition to aggression. He
exhorts you so that you may bear this in mind. (16:90)

Surely it is a sublime Book. No falsehood can ever enter
it from before nor behind; it is a bestowal from on high
by the One who is All-Wise, ever due to Him all praise.
(41:41–42)

It is of great significance that the religion of Islam is founded
upon the Qur'an and that all Muslims see this book as the final
authority. The Qur'an occupies a position in Islamic civilization
similar to the place held by the Constitution within American
society. People may debate its meaning and interpret it according to their own views, but finally when they want to establish
justice, claim their rights, or justify their actions, they will refer
to it. But only a small part of the Qur'an refers to legal or social
issues; the greater portion of it is for spiritual guidance.

The Qur'an is not believed to be the voice of Muhammad,
but a voice from beyond the human realm. Yet it is addressed
to the essential needs of human beings, reminding them of
their essential nature, their moral responsibilities, and of the
exquisite grace and guidance that the Divine showers upon humanity. It is also full of warning about the ways in which human beings can harm themselves, each other, their world, and
finally their own souls.

Muhammad had a voice, too, and his pithy and wise sayings

were remembered and recorded, eventually becoming a supple-
mentary source of Islamic practice and conduct. And yet the
voice of Muhammad remains indistinct from the voice of the
Qur'an. Muhammad's character and behavior became a model
for all Muslim behavior, and his conduct and manner of worship became the model of Islamic practice and spirituality. In
fact this model has remained so powerful and alive that when
the great German poet Rilke visited Egypt in 1900, he ob-
served that the memory of Muhammad was so present, it was
as if he had died only last week. Here is some of what the
Qur'an says about the Prophet Muhammad:

> [He] enjoins upon them [his followers] the doing of what
> is right and forbids them the doing of what is wrong, and
> makes lawful to them the good things of life and forbids
> the bad and impure things, and lifts from them their bur-
> dens and the shackles that have been upon them. It is
> those who believe in him, and honor him, and support
> him and follow the light which was sent down with him,
> it is they who will attain to success. (7:157)

The Qur'an and the Prophet exert a powerful influence over
the Muslim faithful. Islam's basic tenets and daily practice are
more or less agreed upon by the vast majority of Muslims.
Whether Shia, Sunni, or Sufi, they read the same holy book,
they worship, fast, and make a pilgrimage in the same way. And
yet we cannot tell you exactly what Islam is. There is no single
religious authority, and it is too broad and deep to be captured
in mere concepts and words. Nevertheless, we will do our best
to describe some of the basics of this faith and what it feels like
to live in an Islamic universe.

There is today a struggle for the meaning of Islam: who will speak for it, what it stands for, and what its essential values are. This book will attempt to present and illuminate the main sources that have guided Islamic civilization for fourteen centuries. It will also to some extent describe the prevailing way of life actually lived by the vast majority of Muslims around the world, for, despite the wide range of cultures embraced by Islamic civilization, there is an identifiable Muslim character and culture that runs through all of them. That is part of Islam's remarkable power. That it has held together with such coherence and cohesion for fourteen centuries is evidence of the power of its inspiration and guiding sources. Yet, inevitably, there is a discrepancy between the ideal of any religion and its actuality. We should keep in mind that extreme deviations from the normative Islam might exist.

Bear in mind that Islam is more a way of life than a theology. Muslims are in agreement on what the basic practices are: they offer essentially the same prayers at the same times, fast in the same way, and read the same Holy Book. This accounts for a high degree of similarity across diverse cultures. Furthermore, Islam touches upon every aspect of life—not only worship and religious ceremony, but economics, conjugal and family relations, diet, hospitality, art, and science.

In the domain of beliefs, the propositions are also relatively few and simple. There is one God who has sent countless messengers to humanity, of which Muhammad is the last, confirming the truth of previous messengers. As human beings, we will be accountable here and hereafter for our actions, and what matters most is our mindfulness of God (*taqwa*) and the goodness of our actions.

The Qur'an and the sayings of Muhammad address the human condition with certain proposals about what is of ultimate importance, what human well-being consists of, what kinds of mistakes human beings have made, and how we have harmed ourselves, each other, and our environment. Its central message, however, is essentially this: to keep God at the center of one's consciousness, or, in other words, to be thankful, aware, just, patient, forgiving, and generous in God's name.

"Islam" actually means "submission," and Islam is at its heart the submission of the human being to God. The Arabic root word, *islam*, is, however, related to *salam*, which means "peace" and/or "security." Thus, Islam can be defined as the attainment of inner peace and security through submission to God. Yet Islam is hardly a dictatorship of the Divine. Islam holds that, since God is the Creator and Sustainer of the universe, it is only natural that our own well-being has something to do with being in relationship with the Divine. A Muslim is one who consciously submits to the divine order. In a sense, every living being on earth, and everything that exists, is "muslim" insofar as it is subject to the laws of nature, which are part of the divine order.

Human beings are in a unique position, however, for with us this submission is left as a voluntary act. We have the free will to live either in faith and submission or in denial and resistance.

The Qur'an describes three categories of human beings: the faithful, the deniers, and the hypocrites. The first two categories are usually mistranslated as "believers" and "unbelievers." The reason these are inadequate translations is that "faith," in the Islamic sense of the word, cannot be equated with "belief." Faith has more to do with an inner conviction of the heart, a sense of the meaningful order of existence and the beneficence of the Divine. The faithful have this conviction. A saying of the Prophet Muhammad defines "faith" in this way: "Faith is a confession of the tongue, a verification with the heart, and an action with the body."

The deniers, on the other hand, willfully turn their backs on the Divine and aggressively pursue their own self-interest or get lost in their own confusion. The hypocrites, of course, pretend to be faithful while actually being entirely preoccupied with their own self-interest.

The Arabic word for faith is *iman,* and the faithful person is called a *mu'min.* The fundamental meaning of the word is to be in a state of security through having verified for oneself that the Divine can be trusted. The word for denial or misbelief is *kufr* and the denier is the *kafir.* It implies being in denial, covering up, and being ungrateful. These two kinds of people, those who keep faith and those who live in rebellious denial, can be found professing a variety of religious beliefs, including Islam. One's nominal beliefs are not the ultimate saving criteria. According to the Qur'an, a person's spiritual well-being or salvation, to use a Christian term, depends on one's mindfulness of God (*taqwa*) and one's righteous actions (*salihati*).

When the word "Islam" is used in the Qur'an, it is not so much a religion beginning with Muhammad—after all the religion had hardly taken shape yet—but the primordial religion of humanity, the religion of all the prophets that God sent to humanity throughout the ages, beginning with Adam and culminating with Muhammad. In fact, many verses of the Qur'an clearly indicate as much:

> With God, the [only] religion is submission [or "surrender," i.e., Islam]. (3:19)

The Prophet Jacob, upon his deathbed, counseled his sons to follow the faith of his fathers, Islam:

> "O my children! Behold, God has granted you the purest faith; so do not allow death to overtake you before you have submitted yourselves unto Him."
>
> Nay, but you [yourselves, O children of Israel] bear witness that when death was approaching Jacob, he said unto his sons: "Whom will you worship after I am gone?"
>
> They answered: "We will worship your God, the God of your forefathers Abraham and Ishmael and Isaac, the One God; and unto Him will we surrender ourselves." (2:132–133)

The Arabic text of this verse has the Prophet Jacob telling his children, literally, "then die not except in a state of submission [to God]." The apostles of Jesus also bore witness that they followed the religion of Islam, i.e., they submitted themselves to God:

> And when Jesus became aware of their refusal to acknowledge the truth, he asked: "Who will be my helpers in God's cause?"
>
> The white-garbed ones [Jesus' disciples] replied: "We shall be your helpers in the cause of God! We are faithful to God: and may you bear witness that we have submitted ourselves unto Him!" (3:52)

Again, the literal translation is "bear witness that we are in submission." The particulars of submission have differed according to time and place, but the core message of Islam preached by every prophet was the same:

> Their brother Salih said unto them: "Will you not be conscious of God? Behold, I am a prophet [sent by Him] to you, worthy of your trust: be, then, conscious of God, and pay heed unto me!
>
> "And no reward whatever do I ask of you for it: my reward rests with none but the Sustainer of all the worlds." (26:142–145)

As the last of the Abrahamic faiths to arrive on the scene, Islam sees itself as the final culmination of the message of all the prophets.

A MEETING WITH GABRIEL

An event that is enshrined in Muslim memory from the time of the Prophet Muhammad will help us to understand the cardinal points of Islamic faith and practice. Here is the story as it is recorded in an early collection of the Prophet's sayings, Sahih Bukhari:

> One day the Prophet came out before the people gathered to meet him, and a man came up to him and said: "What is faith [*iman*]?"
>
> He replied: "Faith means that you have faith in God, His angels, His Books, in [your] meeting Him, in His prophets, and in the Resurrection."
>
> Then he asked: "What is *islam*?"

He answered: "*Islam* is that you worship God and don't associate anything with Him, that you perform the prayer [*salah*], give in charity, and fast during the month of Ramadan."

Then he asked: "What is the most beautiful conduct [*ihsan*]?"

He replied: "To worship and serve God as though you see Him. And even if you don't see Him, surely He sees you."

Then he went off, and the Prophet said: "Bring him back." But they couldn't find him. Then he said: "That was Gabriel, who came to teach the people their Religion [*din*]."

This story succinctly presents three dimensions of the religion of Islam. The idea of a distinct religion named Islam is a concept that was developed gradually over the course of the twenty-three years during which the Qur'an was gradually revealed. In the earliest revelations the word *din,* here translated as religion, has a wider, more universal dimension. It suggests a very fundamental relationship with the Divine, and the beliefs and practices that go with it. *Din* also carries the sense of a reckoning. In other words, it initially meant the bottom line, what a human life adds up to, the fundamental value of one's existence. In other words, if we fail to include the eternal, spiritual dimension into our accounting, it will be way off. We will have missed the point of life.

Here, however, the religion that is being taught is addressed to the community of Muhammad, summarizing all that has been revealed and all that is expected of the faithful.

The passage begins with a description of the basic spiritual context, *iman* (faith), then describes the essential practice, *islam*, and ends with the most essential, i.e. spiritual, understanding of the whole matter, *ihsan*, a word whose root meaning suggests conducting oneself in both the most righteous and beautiful manner. The reference in the hadith, or prophetic utterance, is certainly to the Qur'anic usage of the term, where "those who do *ihsan*" are referred to at least twenty-five times with the highest praise. Even more strikingly, the Qur'an insists that "verily God is with those who act in awareness of Him and the *muhsinun* [righteous]" (16:128; 29:69); "Do *ihsan*, truly God loves the *muhsinun*" (2:195). God's profoundest Love (*hubb*) is given to them and this is repeated in 3:134, 3:148, 5:13, 5:93; and "God's Lovingkindness (*rahma*) is near to the *muhsinun*" (7:56).

One subtle but essential point to grasp is that these terms can be applied in two contexts: the universal and the sectarian. There is, for instance, *islam*, the state of being reconciled with and surrendered to God. This *islam* (intentionally with a small "i") is the nature of true religion everywhere and always. This is described in the early verse: "Indeed with God [the only] religion is self-surrender [*islam*]." Then there is "Islam," the religion of the particular community of Muhammad, a concept that was introduced in the last revelations of the Qur'an, when God says, "And as of today I have perfected your religion for you and it is Islam." Most Muslims are aware of the dual meaning of these words, and even the most orthodox would grant this scope to the term.

As for the term *iman*, as we have said it suggests the personal verification of the spiritual dimension of reality. Faith is known by the heart and then acted upon. And a verse in the Qur'an suggests that faith (*iman*) is actually a higher or deeper state than *islam*. For instance, in verse 49:14, God instructs the Prophet to tell the Bedouin Arabs that:

> You have not attained to faith; you should rather say, 'We have [outwardly] surrendered' for faith has not yet entered your hearts. But if you pay heed unto God and His Apostle, He will not let the least of your deeds go to waste: for, behold, God is much-forgiving, a dispenser of grace.

Perhaps there is no better summation of the faith than this Qur'anic *ayah*:

> The Prophet, and the faithful with him, have faith in what has been bestowed upon him from on high by his Sustainer: they all believe in God, and His angels, and His revelations, and His prophets, making no distinction between any of His prophets; and they say:
> "We have heard, and we pay heed. Grant us Your forgiveness, O our Sustainer, for with You is all journeys' end! (2:285)

The faith has these basic cornerstones: 1) God; 2) angels; 3) God's prophets; 4) God's revelations; 5) the reckoning and afterlife; and 6) divine destiny and decree.

1. *God*

First and foremost is the recognition of an absolute Divine Being: God, the Creator and Sustainer of the Universe. The Qur'an enumerates many qualities, or attributes, of God, of which these six are thought to be primary: God is living, knowing, seeing, and hearing, and God wills (or acts) and communicates. He is the Creator, the Giver of Life. This is the God of Adam, Seth, Noah, Abraham, Moses, and Jesus, and indeed the God of all religions. The short, often repeated Surah Ikhlas gives the most succinct and comprehensive expression of the nature of the Divine to be found in the Qur'an:

> Say: "He is the One God: God the Eternal, Uncaused Cause of All That Exists. He begets not, and neither is He begotten; and there is nothing that could be compared with Him."

It could also be translated in another way:

> Say: "God is One, the Eternally Self-Subsistent, upon whom everything depends, Who was neither born nor gives birth, and nothing is comparable to this One."

From the very beginning the Qur'an has made its central theme the recognition and love of God. On one hand, as the above chapter informs us, nothing can be compared to God, no description, no theology, no human formulation can encompass the reality of God, and at the same time "He is nearer to you than your jugular vein."

The very first revelation Muhammad received while on retreat in a cave on Mount Hira is not a message of utter transcendence, but an expression of generous love to humankind:

> *Read, in the name of your Sustainer who created.*
> *Created the human being from a clinging substance.*
> *Read, for truly your Sustainer is the Most Generous*

Who taught with the Pen (of Divine Intelligence),
taught the human being what it did not know.

The word here translated as Sustainer is *rabb,* and it is from the same root as the Hebrew word for rabbi. Although it has commonly been translated with the biblical "Lord," it has the essential meaning of educating, nurturing, and sustaining. These verses describe a relationship between a generous, creative educator and the human being. So the very first revelation encourages the human being to "read" or "recite," a command both to perceive, as in *reading,* and to bring forth something from within ourselves, as in *reciting.*

Among the most important facts to understand about Islam is that it is rigorously monotheistic: there can be only one God, fully unique and sovereign. No one can share in the Godhood. Thus, Islam does not accept the divinity of Jesus and rejects the notion of the Christian Trinity (God the Father, Son, and Holy Spirit). The Qur'an makes this unequivocally clear: "People of scripture [Christians], do not go to excess in your religion, and do not say anything about God but the truth. The Messiah Jesus son of Mary was only a messenger, a word, from God, which God sent down to Mary, a spirit from God. So believe in God and God's messengers. And do not speak of a trinity; it is best for you to refrain. God is one of sole divinity, too transcendent to have a son, in possession of all in the heavens and on earth. And God is a good enough patron" (4:171).

The Arabic name for God, and the name that Muslims use to call him, is *Allah.* There are those who claim that *Allah* is not the Judeo-Christian God, but the God of Muhammad alone. However, Arab Christians and Jews also use the name *Allah* for God. When we and our Arab Christian friends part, we fre-

quently say to each other, *Allah ma'akum,* or "God be with you."
Translations of the Bible into Arabic use the term *Allah* for
God.

The word *Allah* itself comes from the same root as the words
used for God in the Bible: *Elohim, ha Elohim,* and *ha Eloh Allah*
also comes from the same root word for God in the Aramaic/
Syriac language, the language spoken by Jesus, which is *Alaha.*
The word *Elohim* is derived from the Hebrew *eloh,* which means
"god." The *im* that is appended to the end of *eloh* is a plural of
abstraction, appended for respect. It is like the "royal we" used
by kings and others wishing to glorify themselves in the English
language. The Aramaic *Alaha* is the emphatic form of *alah,*
which is Aramaic for "god." Similarly, *Allah* is connected to the
Arabic word *ilah,* which also means "divinity." These three
words—*eloh, alah, ilah*—are etymologically equivalent, just as
Deus, Dios, and *Dio* are equivalent names for God in Latin,
Spanish, and Italian, respectively. The proto-Semitic root for
these *eloh, alah,* and *ilah* is *'LH,* which means "to worship."
Thus, the literal meaning of the words *Elohim, Alaha,* and *Allah*
is "the one who is worshipped." In the Shema, the most important Jewish devotional phrase, the Hebrew says, *Adonai Elohaynu,* which means "the Lord is our God." *Adonai* means "my
Lord," and the *aynu* means "our," and thus *Elohaynu* can be
translated as "our *Eloh,*" again very similar to "our *Allah.*"

In the New Testament, there are two verses that we believe
also contain *Allah:* Matthew 27:46 and Mark 15:34. In Matthew,
Jesus cries: *Eli, Eli, lama sabachthani?* and in Mark, Jesus again
cries: *Eloi, Eloi, lama sabachthani?* Both are translated to mean,
"My God, my God, why hast thou forsaken me?" The words
Eli and *Eloi* are derivations of the word *El,* which is another ver-
sion of *Allah.*

There are some Muslims who believe that the Creator should not be referred to as "God," citing *Allah* as the only "true" proper name for God. The word "God," however, is a beautiful prehistoric word, dating back to at least the Neolithic period. It is derived from the proto-Indo-European root word *gheu*, which means "to invoke" or "to supplicate." In fact, the word "God" is a past participle (forgive our delving into a bit of grammar here), and thus it means "the one who is invoked" or "the one who is called upon." It is very similar to the meaning of the words *Elohim*, *Alaha*, and *Allah*. The English word "God" dates back to before Christianity and its earliest documented use is in the poem *Beowulf*. This poem is the oldest in the English language and is the earliest European vernacular epic. Therefore, anyone who claims that the word "God" is not an authentic name for the Creator is ignorant of the word itself and has no understanding of how ancient and beautiful the word "God" truly is.

To claim that the only name for God is *Allah* speaks of an attitude of cultural bias that is not appropriate for a Muslim. Islam is a religion that explicitly acknowledges that God has sent prophets and messengers to all communities on earth and revealed to them a basic spiritual truth *in their own tongue*. The names for God throughout human history and among the various peoples of the earth have varied: the ancient Egyptians used words such as *Sha'*, *Khabkhab*, and *Nehef*. The ancient Chinese used the term *Shang Ti*. The people of ancient India used the words *Dhatr* and *Prjapati*. The ancient English word for the Creator was "God," and for those of us born and raised American, this is the term we use for God in our everyday speech.

There are relatively few things in Islam that are absolute,

and belief in God is one of these. One cannot be a Muslim without a firm and unwavering faith in God.

2. *Angels*

The Qur'an also mentions angels. These are often envisioned as creatures of light whose sole purpose is to serve and worship God. Angels deeply permeate Muslim belief, theology, and scripture. According to the Qur'an, there are angels who support the throne of God; others surround the throne of God; others sing the praises of God. There is an angel charged with taking the souls of those destined to die: the angel of death, Azraeel. There is another angel, Israfeel, charged with blowing a trumpet to herald the day of judgment. Two angels are mentioned by name in the Qur'an, Gabriel and Michael. The archangel Gabriel is the angel of revelation, bringing verses of scripture from God to his messengers. Michael is one of the archangels of God.

There are angels who write down every deed of every human being and record them in a book, and there are angels charged with guarding every human being: "There are guardians over you, honorable, keeping records, who know what you do" (82:10–12). After a person dies, two angels will visit the grave to ask about the life he or she has led. Angels cannot but serve and follow the command of God, because they were created thus. Consequently, the notion of angels who "rebelled" against God—as some Christians believe—is foreign to Muslims.

3–4. *Prophets and Revelations*

Muslims acknowledge a history of revelation on this earth and on principle accept all of God's books and scriptures. We believe these holy scriptures were sent from God to humanity to guide us in our daily lives. In fact God's foremost act of mercy is this communication with humanity through divine revelation. The words are those of God, but the messenger is merely human. The Prophet Muhammad said that the verses revealed to him were as if "written upon his heart." Muslims believe that scriptures were first sent to humanity through Seth, the son of Adam, and they culminated in the revelation given to the Prophet Muhammad, the Qur'an.

Muslims accept the sacred nature of all previous revelations, although they give special credence to the Qur'an because it was the only scripture revealed in the clear light of historical time, and because it is thought to be free of human tampering. Since Muslims accept all the scriptures of God, it follows that they must also acknowledge all the prophets sent by God. The prophets are human beings specially chosen to guide humanity toward God's path. The first prophet was Adam, the first human created by God, the father of humanity. The last of the prophets is Muhammad, the Prophet of Islam. From among the prophets an even more elite group is recognized—the messengers, those who were charged to bring a holy book to their peoples. These include: Seth, Abraham (the scrolls of Abraham), Moses (the Torah), David (the Psalms), Jesus (the Gospel), and Muhammad (the Qur'an). The Qur'an mentions twenty-five prophets by name; these include Adam, Noah, Abraham, Isaac, Ishmael, Enoch, Jonah, Jacob, Joseph, Moses, David, Solomon, and Jesus. What is interesting about the prophets in the Qur'an is that Moses and Jesus are mentioned by name many times more than the Prophet Muhammad himself. The Qur'an sums it up perfectly: "We believe in God, and in what has been revealed to us, and in what was revealed to Abraham, Ishmael, Isaac, Jacob, and the Tribes; and in what was given to Moses, Jesus, and the prophets, from their Lord. We do not discriminate between individuals among them; for we submit to God" (3:84).

5. *The Reckoning and Afterlife*

During a visit to an Islamic country, you will often see a grocer weigh out a kilo of cherries for instance, and then some. Once, after a friend of ours left some fifty-dollar bills in a shirt he brought to the laundry, the bills were found paper-clipped to the clean shirt. Muslims have an acute sense of eternal accountability. This has less to do with being terrified by some hypothetical judgment day and more to do with the notion of *taqwa*, a term that's impossible to translate exactly, but let's try. *Taqwa* has to do with guarding oneself from the negative effects of our own heedlessness. In the words of one imam, "It is the state you might feel if you walked into a room and saw an infant sleeping on the floor—the care you would take not to step on the baby, nor even to wake it, that is *taqwa*." *Taqwa* is a vigilant awareness about doing the right thing. It is moral fastidiousness, and in Islam it is the most important criterion determining our relationship with God.

For those of us who are not impressed by such a fastidious and nuanced ethical sense, well, then, there's a more dramatic scenario. The Qur'an describes in vivid and tangible terms the terrible suffering of the Fire, or Jahannum, as it's also called, and the bliss of the Garden, the Qur'anic term for Paradise.

A day will come when all will be made clear, when the consequences of our actions will become apparent. Those with *taqwa* will be well prepared, but those of us who were accustomed to living in denial, pursuing the fulfillment of our selfish desires no matter what the price, will be shocked. "You were unmindful of this Day, now We have removed what covered your vision, and sharp is your sight today" (50:22). On the day of reckoning the people in whose life sins weigh heavy will even want to disown those whom they associated with, both their leaders and those who followed along with them.

> Lost indeed are they who consider it a lie that they will have to meet God—till the Last Hour suddenly comes upon them, and they cry, "Alas for us, that we disregarded it!"—for they shall bear on their backs the burden [of their sins]: oh, how evil the load with which they shall be burdened! And the life of this world is little more than a play and a passing delight; and the life in the hereafter is by far the better for all who are conscious of God. Will you not, then, use your reason? (6:32)

> On that Day it will come to pass that those who had been falsely esteemed shall disown their followers, and the latter shall see the suffering, with all their attachments cut to pieces! And then those followers shall say: "Would that we had a second chance, so that we could disown them as they have disowned us!" Thus will God show them their works as bitter regrets; but they will not come out of the fire. (2:166–167)

Islam, like Christianity, does not take this earthly life as an end in itself. While there is a great deal of teaching and guidance about how to live a good life, human beings are constantly reminded of a much larger context. The Qur'an constantly forces the reader, or listener, to shift perspective, to expand one's awareness to include eternity: "Did you then think that We created you in mere idle play, and that you would not return to Us?" (23:115).

Every human being is accountable to God for his or her actions and intentions. "Every person's fate is fastened to their neck and on the Day of Resurrection, We shall bring out an open book, saying, 'Read your own book. You, yourself, can sufficiently read it' " (17:13–14).

Some claim this is the cause of the "culture of death" with which Islam imbues its followers, by which we mean an incessant focus by some Muslims on paradise and the life after death. This has been brought up especially in relation to suicidal Muslim militants who strap bombs on their chests and murder innocent people so that they can have "seventy-two virgins" in paradise.

But Islam's vivid end-time theology doesn't exist so that Muslims can blow themselves up. Instead, Islam exhorts its followers to live a righteous life on earth.

For example, the eighty-third chapter of the Qur'an begins with this passage: "Woe to the cheaters, who demand full measure when they receive from people, but short them when they measure or weigh for them. Don't they think they'll be resurrected for a trying day, the day when humankind will stand before the Lord of the universe?" (83:1–6). This means that a Muslim businessman who is cognizant of the afterlife would never even fathom misstating company earnings in order to inflate the stock price and line his pockets with ill-gained money. He would always remember God's question: "Do they not think that they will be called to account?" On Judgment Day, all scores will be settled; all disputes will be mediated; all injustices will be corrected.

The presence of evil in the world makes the existence of a final day of reckoning a necessity. If we believe that God is ulti-mately just, it is impossible for so much injustice to exist in the world without some accountability. This does not mean Mus-lims must simply acquiesce to any injustice they see. Far from it. Islam demands Muslims right any injustice toward any hu-man being, Muslim or otherwise, as mentioned by verses of the Qur'an such as this one: "Believers, be supporters of justice, as witnesses to God, even if it be against yourselves, or your parents or relatives; whether one be rich or poor" (4:135). If Muslims shirk this responsibility, then corruption will be wide-spread on the earth. In fact, if Muslims fail to fight injustice, they will be called to account by God for this failure on the day of judgment. Therefore, an injustice against anyone anywhere is an affront to every Muslim everywhere.

Since the hereafter is so strongly focused upon in Islam, the faith has a rich and colorful belief system about the end-time that includes angels, trumpets, terror, and fire. The Qur'an de-clares: "Their reckoning has drawn near for humanity, yet they turn away in heedlessness" (21:1). The day of judgment has signs, and the prophetic traditions are full of various events that must occur before the end of days. Many have come true, and others are yet to be fulfilled. In Muslim belief, the day of judg-ment will be preceded by a trumpet blast made by the angel Is-rafeel. This blast will render dead all that was alive, including the angels. The only one left will be God, who will then raise Israfeel from the dead, and he will blow on the trumpet a sec-ond time, which will herald the final day. For those who did not live righteous lives, the Qur'an tells us, it will be a day of un-imaginable terror. In fact, it is this day that guides the conduct of Muslims on earth. For example, the Prophet Muhammad told us that on the last day, there will be someone who will have an enormous amount of good deeds, yet he had cursed and harmed some people during his life. These people will then come to him asking for their retribution. The only thing he can give them is his good deeds, and when they run out, the sins of those he harmed will be given to him. As a result, he will be condemned to hell. This story expresses the utmost importance of being good to others on earth, because we will be accountable. The Qur'an is full of vivid imagery of the day of judgment, to constantly remind us that we will be brought forth before God for judgment. This is one such passage:

> When the sun is rolled up, and when the stars fall lusterless, and when the mountains are blown away, and when the pregnant camels are neglected, and when the wild beasts are herded, and when the oceans are flooded, and when the souls are matched, and when the infant girl who was buried alive is asked for what offense she was killed: And when the pages are opened, and when the sky is stripped, and when the blaze is fired up, and when Paradise is brought near, each soul will know what it has brought about. (81:1–14)

These verses are read both in the ritual prayers (about which more will be said below) and personally by Muslims in their homes and mosques.

On the day of judgment, Muslims believe everybody receives a book recording their deeds on earth—the writings of the angels who sit on the shoulders of each person. People who get the book presented to them in their right hand are sent to a life of eternal bliss in paradise. If, on the other hand, the book of deeds is presented behind the person's back in the left hand, the person will cry: "Oh, if only I hadn't been handed my record and never knew what my account was. Oh, if only that had been the end! My property has been of no avail to me, my power has passed away from me" (69:25–29). Then, the command of God will be given: *"Seize him and bind him, and let him burn in the blaze"* (69:30–31). Yet, how the book of deeds is presented is not the criterion for judgment by God. God is more just than that. The deeds will be weighed on scales: good deeds on one side, and bad ones on the other. If the good deeds outweigh bad deeds, the end is paradise. If bad deeds outweigh the good, then hell is the final abode. This, however, does not mean that the condemned will be in hell for eternity. There are many who will be punished for a time, and then taken out of hell and placed in heaven. Given that the stakes are so high, belief in the day of judgment is essential to the theology of every Muslim, and it permeates everyday life. Many Muslims take the verses and prophetic traditions describing the happenings of Judgment Day literally, but some believe that the verses describing the terrors of Judgment Day are allegorical. Whether they are taken literally or not is immaterial, the point of the verses is to constantly remind us that we will be called to account by God for our actions here on earth.

6. *Divine Destiny and Decree*

Muslims live within a universe where the will of God is ever present, and this is reflected in the language they use. Indeed, when most Muslims talk about the future, they do not do so unless they say, *"Insha'Allah,"* or "if God wills." When they see a beautiful child, they say, *"Mash'Allah,"* thanks be to God, and whenever anything good or bad happens, they are likely to say, *"Alhamdulillah,"* praise be to God. This does not mean that

Muslims believe they are predestined and have no free will. Human beings have a certain degree of free will, and they must live with the consequences of their actions. Sometimes things happen beyond a person's control, and one must be patient. In fact, there is a phrase Muslims are taught to say when something does not go their way: "God has decreed thus, and he does what he wills." That being said, this does not absolve someone of personal responsibility. If a Muslim does not lock his car and it gets stolen, yes, God did decree that the car be stolen, but that does not get the Muslim off the hook for not locking the car. "Trust in God but tether your camel first," the Prophet Muhammad advised.

The word for destiny in Arabic, *qadr*, suggests God's power and a measuring out. A beneficent measuring and proportion governs our lives, and a person of faith trusts that this is for the good of their souls. As for the ultimate question of resolving the true meaning of destiny and how we can have free will if what is going to happen will happen, the Prophet Muhammad simply said, "Destiny is a secret with God, which neither humans nor angels fully comprehend."

2

THE FIVE PILLARS

For non-Muslims, the Five Pillars are perhaps the one element of the faith they have some familiarity with—even if it's just the term. But what are they—and why are they called pillars? They are called pillars because the Prophet once remarked: "Islam is built upon five things." These five things are elements of practice that stand in addition to the elements of belief we discussed earlier, and they are: 1) *shahadah*, or witnessing; 2) *salah*, or worship; 3) fasting; 4) *zakat*, or charity; and 5) *hajj*, or pilgrimage.

1. *The* Shahadah, *or Witnessing*

The first of the Five Pillars is the most important in Islam, the *shahadah*. It is a declaration that there is no god worthy of worship except God (the God of Abraham and, indeed, all religions), and that Muhammad is his messenger and servant. The Arabic phrase goes as follows: *La illaha il Allah, Muhammadan Rasulullah.* This declaration is uttered in public whenever someone chooses to become a Muslim. *Shahadah* means "the witnessing." The words of the *shahadah* are the essence of

Islam; every concept of the faith stems from this phrase. To bear witness that nothing is worthy of worship except God affirms the conviction that 1) there is a God, 2) this God is the Creator and Sustainer of the Universe, and 3) as such, he alone is deserving of worship and trust. The effect of this mindful witnessing is to help us remember that we come from God and to God we will return. As the Qur'an says:

> O you who have faith! Be mindful of God with all the mindfulness that is due Him, and do not allow death to overtake you before you have surrendered yourselves to Him.
>
> And hold fast, all together, to the rope of God, and do not draw apart from one another.
>
> And remember with gratitude the blessings which God has bestowed on you: how, when you were adversaries, He brought your hearts together, so that through His blessings you became as though of one family; and how when you were on the brink of a fiery abyss, He saved you from it. In this way, God makes clear His signs to you, so that you might be guided, and that there might grow out of you a community that invites to all that is good, and encourages the doing of what is right and forbids the doing of what is wrong; and it is they who shall attain happiness! (3:102–104)

So the *shahadah* is an expression of love for God. If one affirms that nothing is worthy of worship except God, then we can love nothing else more than God. This love is manifested by gratitude, remembrance, and a willingness to live according to divine guidance. If we believe nothing is worthy of worship except God, then we cannot fathom blatantly disobeying God. If we sin, which we're bound to do, then we return to God and ask for forgiveness.

The second part of the declaration, "and Muhammad is his messenger and servant," is related to the first. Once someone accepts that nothing is worthy of worship except God, he or she will respect all of God's prophets and messengers and especially the one who brought this last revelation to humanity. Muslims try to follow his example to the best of their ability.

Muhammad was a human being. In fact, the old-fashioned term "Mohammedanism" or "Mohammedan" is offensive to Muslims, because the term suggests an inappropriate worship of Muhammad. Muslims worship only God, but they love, revere, and follow Muhammad as their divinely sent prophet. We'll discuss the Prophet much more later in the book.

2. Salah, *or Worship*

The second, and next most important, pillar is the ritual prayer, or *salah* performed five times daily. The times of prayer follow the natural cycle of the sun's daily course. The first prayer, called Fajr, may be offered with the first hint of light at dawn until just before the sun's appearance over the horizon. The second prayer, called Zuhr, is offered just following high noon. Next is Asr, the prayer of the mid-afternoon, followed by Maghrib, immediately after sunset, and finally Isha, which is performed just after dark. Muslim astronomers developed precise methods for calculating the exact times of prayer to be offered in congregation at mosques, and while it is strongly encouraged to perform them as soon as possible, a wider range of time is actually considered permissible.

Salah is not about asking God for anything but about surrendering oneself to the Divine Presence. It is a form of worship with specific rules and motions that engage not only the mind, heart, and spirit, but the body as well. It has elements of mental and audible recitation, a sequence of postures, and perhaps most importantly, a quality of mindfulness encompassing them all. The Prophet Muhammad said, "Salah is not valid without presence," thus once and for all raising it above mere form and ritual. If we are not truly present for this worship, we are not doing it at all, but merely going through the motions, and the motions are not what it's all about. Its primary purpose is to remind one of the presence of God and to demonstrate one's surrender to that presence.

Muslims are encouraged to worship together with others in a mosque when possible. The Prophet said that congregational prayer has great benefit. Still, prayers can be offered alone as well and anywhere on this earth, as the Prophet was reported to have said, "The entire earth has been made a mosque for me." A simple, clean prayer carpet is enough to establish the sacred space of worship. Not only does the location need to be clean, out of respect for the sacred act of approaching the Divine Presence, but the worshipper must also be in a state of "ablution." Therefore, Muslims ritually cleanse themselves prior to offering the prayer. This consists of washing the hands, then the face, then the arms to the elbows, then wiping the fingers over the hair of the head, then washing the feet to the ankles. Each of these is washed three times with fresh cool water. Falling asleep or using the toilet breaks the state of ablution, which should be restored as soon as possible, and at least just before the next prayer. Placing one's feet in the sink may be a bit awkward, especially in the workplace, and, thankfully, there is a provision that allows us to sometimes wipe over our socks and shoes rather than performing the ritual with water, and even, if there is no water available, to use sand, or a stone, or our hands to accomplish the ablution through the intention of purification itself.

This ritual of ablution not only cleanses a Muslim physically, but if accompanied by a pure intention, the purification is moral and spiritual as well. It is understood by most Muslims that the cleansing of these physical parts of ourselves is also a purification of all the ways we may misuse our bodies, including our mouth, head, hands, and feet, through heedless speech, thought, action, and so forth.

The postures of worship are accompanied by specific verses of the Qur'an and other phrases of supplication recited in Arabic. Each of the five times of prayer has a specific number of bowing and prostration cycles: the dawn prayer has two cycles, the noon, late afternoon, and night prayers have four cycles, and the sunset prayer has three cycles. Before each cycle, one faces in the direction of Mecca, raises one's hands up to the side of the head and says in Arabic, "God is greater [than anything]." While standing, we recite the first chapter of the Qur'an, the Fatiha, and then some verses of our own choice. Then, we bow forward, forming a right angle with our upper body and legs. While in this position, we recite three times, "Glory be to my Sustainer, the Almighty." Then standing back up we say, "God hears those who praise him." Then we prostrate ourselves, touching the forehead to the ground. While in this position, we say three times, "Glory be to my Sustainer, the Most High." We then move into a kneeling posture, and then finally prostrate ourselves once more, repeating the glorification as before. After that we stand up for another cycle.

On Fridays, the noon prayer is replaced by the Friday prayer, a special congregational prayer that, according to most Muslims, is obligatory for men. Although women are encouraged to attend, they haven't sinned in the eyes of Islam if they miss Friday prayer. The Friday prayer includes only two cycles instead of four; before the prayer, one of the congregation's leaders delivers a sermon. The event is very similar in tone to Sunday morning church for Christians, or Saturday morning services for Jews. Friday, by the way, is the Sabbath day for Muslims. We're supposed to leave work to attend the Friday prayer. But our Sabbath differs from the Jewish Sabbath, in that after the Friday prayer, we can return to work.

The five prayers we've just described are Islam's only obligatory prayers. During his life, the Prophet offered many more ritual prayers in devotion to God, and so Muslims are encouraged to do the same.

The Qur'an says, "We have laid no excessive burden upon you in matters of religion." And the Prophet, himself, has said, "Woe to anyone who makes the religion [unnecessarily] difficult for others." Islamic practice has made certain allowances for special circumstances. When one is traveling or sick, the prayers can be combined and shortened. So if you're inconveniently on an airplane during prayer time, you can pray the noon and late afternoon prayers together. The same goes for the sunset and night prayers. Furthermore, the Prophet also allowed prayers to be combined (but not shortened) for other legitimate reasons, such as not being able to pray while working. A doctor, for instance, may frequently be unable to pray while making the rounds at the hospital seeing patients. He may instead offer his prayers before the day is finished. That being said, however, combining prayers so that one can watch the Super Bowl undisturbed would probably not be approved by our Prophet were he alive today.

From the point of view of life in the contemporary Western world, the obligation to worship five times a day might seem excessive. Our lives are filled with so many responsibilities and so many distractions. Yet compared to the life of a monk or a yogi, the obligations of a Muslim layman do not appear so onerous. The call to worship five times a day has, however, established among Muslim peoples an abiding awareness of the Divine, a God-centered life, and a social cohesion. In its first centuries the sheer moral vitality and spiritual magnetism of Islamic practice was a civilization-building force.

At its best, when performed with some sincerity, *salah* cuts through our worldly preoccupations and immediately reestablishes a connection with the Divine. It leads us to a state of remembrance of God—a state that ideally should be maintained through our whole lives. The Qur'an says, "And the remembrance of God is the greatest" (29:45). And "Indeed, in the remembrance of God hearts find rest" (13:28).

The ritual prayer is extremely important because it serves to constantly remind the believer that there is a God, and he is in charge. The rat race of life can easily distract us from the greater goal of existence on this earth: to know, remember, and reverence God. The Qur'an says God created human beings in order for them to worship and serve him. Having to pray five times a day, seven days a week, 365 days a year is a powerful reminder of this greater purpose. It helps keep us grounded and prevents us from becoming arrogant. Having to touch your forehead to the ground is a humbling experience, especially when you have to do it day after day.

Through our roles in life, we can get fooled into thinking that we have more power and control than in reality we have. A doctor, for instance, may feel he has the power to give life and take it away. When one stops and prays, bowing and putting one's face to the ground, one is reminded that it is God who gives life and takes it away. We become very grateful for such reminders.

In establishing the daily prayers, the Prophet was continuing the tradition of those who came before him. Studying the Bible, one sees many examples of the prophets bowing before God. For example, Genesis 17:1–3, says: "And when Abram was ninety years old and nine, the Lord appeared to Abram, and said unto him, I am the Almighty God; walk before me, and be thou perfect. And I will make my covenant between me and thee, and will multiply thee exceedingly. And Abram *fell upon his face.*" Jesus, in Matthew 26:39, in the Garden of Gethsemane, before the great trial he was to face, is described in this way: "And he went a little further, and *fell on his face*, and prayed, saying, O my Father, if it be possible, let this cup pass from me: nevertheless not as I will, but as Thou wilt" [emphasis added in both verses].

But ritual prayer is not the only type of prayer in Islam. It is distinguished from *du'a*—supplication, or personal prayers when we call upon God directly from our hearts. This type of prayer was called by the Prophet the "mind of worship." The Qur'an says, "When My servants ask you [O Muhammad] about Me, I am close indeed—I hearken to the prayer of the supplicant when one calls on Me; so let them hearken to Me, and let them believe in Me, and they may go the right way" (2:186). Another verse proclaims: "But your Sustainer says,

'Call on Me, and I will answer you. As for those too self-important to serve Me, they will enter hell abjectly' " (40:60).

Personal prayer is strongly encouraged by Islam—so much so that the Prophet was said to have told one of his Companions, "If you ask for something, ask it of God." When we Muslims pray to God, we affirm that only God is the sustainer of all life in the universe. Only God is able to give everything to everyone at the same time without decreasing his dominion.

Prayer also brings us closer to God. We talk to the Creator, who becomes a loving friend, always there, even if we sometimes forget. According to the Prophet, personal prayer results in one of three outcomes: 1) the prayer is answered immediately, which is what the believer sought in the first place; 2) the answer to the prayer is deferred to the Final Day, when a beautiful recompense will be given; or 3) the prayer blocks a calamity that would have befallen the believer had he not made that prayer.

Ideally a Muslim is someone who is in continual dialogue with God. We believe that remaining aware of our dependence on God is the secret of success, spiritually as well in all aspects of our lives. Prayer is a lifeline. And if our lips sometimes move almost imperceptibly through the course of the day to call upon that One who gave us life in the first place, should it be surprising if our lives seem to be guided and sustained by this inner relationship? This kind of inner, spontaneous prayer is not an obligatory aspect of Islam, but it is the very heart of it. There is a holy saying (in the Hadith Qudsi) by the Prophet in which he relates that God says: "There is nothing that I love more than when my servant seeks to draw near to me through voluntary acts of devotion which cause me to love him or her. And when I love her, I become the seeing with which she sees, the hearing with which she hears, the hand with which she touches, and the feet with which she walks."

3. *Fasting*

You have probably heard of the next pillar of worship in Islam: the annual fast during the month of Ramadan, which is the ninth month in the Islamic calendar. This is a very special month for Muslims. We believe that during the month of Ramadan, on the twenty-seventh night to be exact, the Qur'an began to be revealed to the Prophet Muhammad, when the archangel Gabriel first visited him in the cave of Hira in Mecca. The Qur'an confirms that this even occurred in the month of Ramadan: "O believers, fasting is prescribed for you, as it was prescribed for those before you, that you may be conscientious . . . in the month of Ramadan" (2:183–186). Although this story is one of the most important reasons for the sanctity of Ramadan in the eyes of Muslims, the Qur'an does not say that the fasting ritual itself is connected to this story. The fasting ritual is done so that Muslims can gain God-consciousness, as we will describe below.

Since the Islamic calendar is based on twelve lunar months of thirty days each, Ramadan moves backward by eleven days each year. This system allows the sacred events of the Muslim calendar to progress through the solar year so that they can be experienced in different seasons. Thus, for a few years, Ramadan in the United States occurred in the winter and coincided with the Christmas and Hanukah holiday season. This was nice because everyone had a holiday at the same time. It was even nicer, however, because the days were so short! Why is this important? The fast, you see, consists of abstaining from all food, drink, sexual activity, and even smoking from dawn until sunset for an entire month. During the winter months, dawn is at 6 A.M. and sunset is at 4:30 P.M. Less than twelve hours! But, Ramadan continues to move backward year after year, and eventually it will occur in the summer months, when dawn is at 3:30 A.M., and sunset is at 8:30 P.M.

Although it's not obligatory, Muslims are strongly encouraged, especially in the summer, to wake before dawn and have a small meal to help preserve their strength during the day. The fast can be a bit difficult in the beginning of the month because Muslims are not used to forgoing breakfast for God.

Furthermore, if one is traveling or is sick, one is allowed to break the fast but must make up the missed days at a later date: "Believers! Fasting is prescribed for you, as it was prescribed for those before you, so that you may take precaution, for a certain number of days; but whoever among you is sick or on a journey, then a [like] number of other days" (2:183–184).

Another aspect of Ramadan is gathering to pray as a congregation each night after the last daily prayer. These prayers last well into the night, especially during the summer. Typically the mosque will be packed with worshippers and the mood is almost festive. It feels so great to worship together with hundreds or even thousands of fellow Muslims. These prayers are not obligatory but were strongly encouraged by the Prophet. Although you can perform the prayers alone at home, it is also strongly encouraged to pray them in the mosque with everyone else, and frankly, it does not feel the same if they are not performed that way.

The Ramadan fast serves many purposes. For one thing, it cleanses the body and soul of impurities gathered throughout the year. That's partly because fasting not only encompasses abstention from eating and drinking, but also includes "good conduct" while fasting. We are taught, for instance, that even gossip breaks the fast. The idea is that if we practice restraint during Ramadan, it will carry through the rest of the year. Fasting also teaches patience with the commands of God. We consciously deprive ourselves of sensual pleasures and patiently wait until sunset to enjoy them, for no other reason than for the sake of God. In addition, the fast reminds us of the poor and hungry, and so we are motivated to remember and help the poor and needy through the act of giving charity. In fact, the end of Ramadan is the traditional time for giving a major portion of the charity we offer each year.

Ramadan is a very powerful spiritual experience. It is a chance to "polish the heart," as we try to intensify and deepen our spiritual practices during this month. Ramadan always gives us the spiritual boost we need to help get through the rest of the year. Moreover, the good we try to do, the acts of charity, and even the obligatory Islamic rituals seem to bring more blessings during the month of Ramadan, as if the month were full of the mercy and forgiveness of God. As a result, despite our being deprived of eating and drinking during daylight for thirty days, we always enjoy the month of Ramadan, and we are always sad when it is over.

In addition to Ramadan, the Prophet fasted on certain other days of the year, and he encouraged his followers to do the same, although these fasts aren't obligatory. One of these days is Ashura, the tenth day of the first month of the Islamic calendar. This one day commemorates Noah's sighting of land, the Exodus of the children of Israel from Egyptian bondage, and also the martyrdom of Hussein, the Prophet's noble grandson. Again, like the daily prayers, fasting isn't a practice uniquely created by Muslims; it is an important part of nearly all religious traditions. The Bible is full of references to it: "Then all the children of Israel, and all the people, went up, and came unto the house of God, and wept, and sat there before the Lord, and fasted that day until evening, and offered burnt offerings and peace offerings before the Lord" (Judges 20:26); "Then was Jesus led up of the Spirit into the wilderness to be tempted of the devil. And when he had fasted forty days and forty nights, he was afterward hungered" (Matthew 4:1–2).

4. Zakat, *or Charity*

Muslims must also give a portion of their wealth to the poor. This is called *zakat*, the fourth pillar of Islam, which literally means "purification." This alms tax is one-fortieth, or 2.5 percent, of our accumulated wealth that has been unused for one full year. Although the exact number varies, typically the minimum amount of wealth subject to this tax is $1,200. This wealth has to be unused, and thus the poor are exempt from this tax. Those with debt, such as student loan debt, are also exempt from giving *zakat*. The rules for *zakat* are complex, because wealth, other than cash, such as jewelry, land, crops, and livestock, is also subject to the alms tax. Nevertheless, the basic premise is that "I am my brother's and sister's keeper." Typically, when an American Muslim gives *zakat*, he or she totals all the unused wealth possessed for one year: money in various bank accounts, total value of stocks and other investments, and total value of gold and silver (except that which is worn for personal adornment). The *zakat* due totals 2.5 percent of this amount. Many Islamic websites have *zakat* calculators that make this easier. The money can be given to the mosque, which then discharges it to the poor and needy, or it can be given to charitable organizations, or even directly to individuals in need. Modern Muslim scholars have even allowed *zakat* to be given to non-Muslim nonprofit organizations as well. If someone has needy relatives, the *zakat* should ideally be given to them.

Islam does not shun accumulating wealth; being rich is not a sin in Islam. But we believe that wealth brings responsibility in terms of how we earn the money and how we spend it. In fact, the Qur'an mentions that God has portioned out the sustenance of the poor, at least partly, from the wealth of the rich. In addition, the rich are the last, according to the Prophet, to enter paradise because of the heavy scrutiny placed on how they accumulated and dispersed their wealth. The word *zakat* is fitting for this alms tax, because giving money away every year helps purify both the wealth and the wealthy believer from miserliness and covetousness. It also reminds us once again that God is in charge, and we must submit to his will. Muslims are also strongly encouraged to give even more of their wealth in charity to the less fortunate, over and above the *zakat*. The Prophet did not mention how much this should be; he left it up to the generosity of Muslims themselves. Yet, the Prophet said time and again that this voluntary charity will be rewarded handsomely by God, and he once said, "One's wealth is never decreased by the giving of voluntary charity." This money can be given to any needy person. Another very frequent use of this charity money is for the building and continued support of a mosque or school.

5. *The Hajj, or Pilgrimage*

The last of the five pillars of worship in Islam is the once-in-a-lifetime pilgrimage, the Hajj, to the holy city of Mecca (in modern-day Saudi Arabia). This is an annual event, and each

year about two million Muslims descend upon the holy precincts to fulfill the rituals of the pilgrimage.

The Hajj is a series of rituals that reenact an ancient drama
involving Abraham, his wife Hagar, and their newborn son,
Ishmael. According to the story (found in the book of Genesis
in the Hebrew Bible and in several chapters of the Qur'an),
Abraham was called by God to his service as a prophet to the
people, and Abraham answered immediately. But God tested
Abraham by asking him to abandon his wife and infant son—
the only son born to him after decades—in the barren desert of
Paran. Abraham obeyed. He took his wife and son to Paran
and left them there. As he turned to leave, his wife asked where
he was going. Abraham didn't answer. She asked him again,
and still Abraham did not answer. Hagar then asked, "Did God
order this of you?" "Yes," he replied. Then Hagar said, with
complete faith, "Then He will not let us go astray."

Soon, the food that Abraham had left with his wife and son
ran out, and the baby began to cry from hunger. Hagar searched
desperately for water, running between the two mountains of
Safa and Marwa, but her search was in vain, even though she
ran between both mountains seven times. Finally, when all
hope seemed lost, God intervened, sending the archangel
Gabriel, who struck the earth with the edge of his wing and
miraculously brought a spring of water from the earth. Hagar
returned to her baby son and was surprised to find water where
there was none before. She soon turned the spring into a well.
Later, an Arab tribe migrating from Yemen settled there, paying Hagar for use of the well, which to this day is called Zam-
zam, the name given to it by Arabs.

Later, Abraham returned frequently to visit his son in Paran;
when Ishmael was around thirteen, Abraham had a dream in

which he saw his son sacrificed to God. Not only was the sacrifice of animals to pagan gods commonplace in ancient times, but there were instances of actual human sacrifice as well. At first, Abraham was hesitant, afraid this dream was an evil inspiration. But the dream recurred the next two nights, and this convinced Abraham that it was a command of God. He secretly confided this to his beloved son, who told his father, "Father, do as you are commanded. You shall find me patient."

As Abraham was making his way to the mount to sacrifice his son, Satan met him and tried to dissuade him from his task. Abraham stoned the devil three times. Then, just before Abraham was to sacrifice his son, Ishmael gave his father a last bit of advice: "Father, turn my face away from you so that you do not fail in your task by feeling compassion for me." Abraham did as his son suggested, and struck the knife to his son's neck. The knife, although sharp, did not cut Ishmael's skin. Abraham tried again, but the knife would not cut. Then the Lord called out to Abraham: "O Abraham! You have indeed fulfilled your dream." In Ishmael's stead, God sent Abraham an animal for this sacrifice. In the Bible, the animal is a ram; the Qur'an does not specify what sort of animal it was.

Later on, after this incident, God told Abraham and Ishmael to rebuild the holy house in the barren land of Paran—modern-day Mecca. The first such house in Mecca was originally built by Seth, the third son of Adam. Abraham and Ishmael did as they were told, building a stone edifice dedicated to God. They chose the simplest possible structure, a cube, and this cube is called the Ka'ba. Literally, the word *ka'ba* means "a high place with respect and prestige." The word may also be a derivative of the Arabic word *muka'b,* which means "cube." When you hear about Muslims praying in the direction of Mecca, this is what they are praying toward—an empty cube. If you were to place yourself inside that empty cube, you would be at the point where Muslims from all over the earth face each other.

As noted above, the Ka'ba was first built by Abraham approximately four thousand years ago. Although the Bible mentions the birth of Ishmael and how he lived among the Arabs in Paran, it contains no mention of his building the Ka'ba. The Qur'an tells this story. Also, although the Qur'an does not specifically mention that Ishmael was the son Abraham sacrificed, you can infer this from reading the text. This differs from the biblical text, in which Isaac is sacrificed. One thing must be clear: just because the Qur'an hints that it was Ishmael and not Isaac that was sacrificed, this does not mean that Muslims have any disrespect for Isaac. Muslims love and honor both sons of Abraham.

After Abraham and Ishmael built the Ka'ba, God told Abraham: "And proclaim the Pilgrimage among men: they will come to thee on foot and [mounted] on every kind of camel, lean on account of journeys through deep and distant mountain highways" (22:27). Abraham then stood on a mountain and called into the air for all people to make the Pilgrimage to this house.

Muslims have been responding to the call of Abraham since the days of the Prophet Muhammad, and so the story is close to the heart of every Muslim. Some of it is recounted in the Qur'an; but most of it is passed on in Muslim tradition. The pilgrimage to Mecca should be performed by every able-bodied Muslim adult who is financially able to do so. Thus, the poor are exempt until a way is opened for them. Those who are in debt must first pay off their debt, unless the debtor agrees to a deferment of the payment.

The formal pilgrimage begins when one enters the sacred precincts of Mecca. Prior to entering, the believer must put on two white, unstitched cloths called the *ihram*, which are very similar to towels and can be easily bought anywhere. Many people bring the *ihram* with them, and many travel companies that sponsor Hajj trips provide them for the pilgrims. The pilgrim must be wearing the *ihram* prior to entering the sacred precincts, and there are marked boundaries outside of Mecca where Muslims change into their *ihram*.

Nowadays, some pilgrims change into the *ihram* on the plane to Mecca. It really does not matter where you change. The only requirement is that you enter the sacred precincts wearing the *ihram*. Women wear white clothing and must cover their hair. This is the ultimate equalizer: prince and pauper are indistinguishable. Yet, the *ihram* is more than wearing two white cloths: it is a spiritual state as well. While in this state, the believer must not harm any other living thing, cannot enter into any dispute with a fellow pilgrim, cannot become angry, and cannot engage in sexual relations with his or her spouse. It is a state of total devotion to God. It is also the ultimate test of patience. During the Hajj, there are two million people doing the same thing at the same time, and thus maintaining patience and goodwill toward all fellow pilgrims can be challenging. But that is the point.

Once the Hajji (pilgrim) goes to the Ka'ba, he or she must circumambulate the shrine seven times in a counterclockwise direction in the tradition of Abraham, who is said to have started this practice. The number seven was chosen by Abraham. A prayer is offered with each circuit around the holy shrine. After this, a short prayer is offered behind the Station of Abraham, a niche that is said to house an imprint of Abraham's footprints. It is believed that Abraham stood at that place to make sure the construction of the Ka'ba was sound. He would stand there for hours, and thus his feet became imprinted in the sand. After this, the believer then runs between the mountains of Safa and Marwa seven times, just as Hagar did centuries earlier, as she urgently searched for water for her baby.

The pilgrims then move to the tent city of Mina, three miles to the east of Mecca, spending the night in preparation for the most important day of the Hajj: standing on the plain of Arafat the next morning. The name "Arafat" comes from the Arabic word meaning "to know or recognize." Here, according to tradition, Adam and Eve met after their expulsion from the garden of Eden. On this same plain two million pilgrims dressed in simple, white cloths, as if in a dress rehearsal for the day of reckoning, stand before their God and ask for mercy. At the end of the day, we believe, every sin of ours is forgiven. The slate is wiped clean, and the pilgrim is reborn.

Then, following Arafat, pilgrims spend the night in the open air on the plain of Muzdalifah, where they individually gather seven stones each in preparation for the next morning. At that time, in Mina, they symbolically stone a pillar in commemoration of Abraham's stoning of the devil as the devil tried to dissuade him from sacrificing his son. There are actually three pillars, but pilgrims stone only the largest, following the Prophet Muhammad's tradition. After this pillar is stoned, pilgrims once more circle the Ka'ba seven times and make one last run between Safa and Marwa. After this is completed, most of the men shave their heads, and the women cut off some locks of their hair, and then they change out of the *ihram* garb and into their personal clothes.

They spend the next three days in the tent city of Mina, worshipping God in their tents and stoning the three pillars representing the devil. Pilgrims then make one last circumambulation of the Ka'ba just before they leave the holy city of Mecca.

In Islam travel itself is a religious obligation. Not only is the Hajj a central ritual, but the Qur'an frequently enjoins the faithful to see the world and also to reflect on what has happened to societies that lost sight of the balance that a just and righteous life entails. Ever since the advent of Islam, Muslims from all over the world have traveled to Mecca annually, not only encountering an awesome experience of the Divine, but also mixing with people of other lands, and exchanging cultural and scientific knowledge. No one can accurately estimate the profound positive effect this has had on Muslim and other societies. It is one of the generous side effects of the Hajj. Trade routes were established through a large part of the civilized world, and in communities everywhere some made the arduous journey of a lifetime, returning not only with spiritual renewal but with goods, new experiences, and knowledge. Many Americans, for instance, may remember the effect that the Hajj had on Malcolm X, leader of the so-called Black Muslims, transforming him from a racist cult leader into a man who embraced all races and appreciated the altruistic and humanitarian values that Islam, ideally, stands for. Over the centuries, the Hajj helped to create a more unified Islamic civilization, and yet a civilization that was neither insular nor parochial, but an expression of the universal values of Islam.

As was mentioned previously the rituals of the Hajj are

based upon the story of the Prophet Abraham. Yet, his importance to Islam extends beyond the Hajj. Abraham made a
prayer to God: "Our Lord, I have settled some of my children
in a valley without crops near Your sacred House, our Lord,
that they may keep up prayer: so make the hearts of some people fond of them, and provide them with fruits, that they may
be grateful" (14:37). The answer to this prayer came in the
form of a tribe from Yemen that settled in Mecca and provided
Hagar with her sustenance. Ishmael grew up among this tribe
and eventually became the progenitor of the Arab people. In
addition, as Abraham and Ishmael were building the Ka'ba,
they made this prayer: "And send them a messenger from
among them, who will declare Your signs to them, and teach
them scripture and wisdom, and purify them: for You are most
powerful, most wise" (2:129). This prayer went unanswered
until the year 570 c.e., when one of Ishmael's direct descendants was born in the selfsame city of Mecca. The child's name
was Muhammad, which means "the praised one," and this child
was destined to become one of the most important men in human history.

MUHAMMAD

Messenger of God

Without the character of Muhammad, the early Muslim community would not have possessed the magnetic and inspired qualities that gave birth to a high level of culture. Within a few generations, this impulse of Islam spread from the backwaters of Arabia to become a vast civilization—a civilization based on a universal ideology of human equality, social justice, and divine remembrance.

Without the character of Muhammad, who was called "the living Qur'an," the whole spirit of Islamic civilization is inconceivable. The study of the Prophet's sayings and actions has always been central to Islam. Ali, one of the Prophet's closest Companions, preserved these words, which he heard from the Prophet Muhammad:

> *Meditation in God is my capital.*
> *Reason and sound logic are the root of my action.*
> *Love is the foundation of my existence.*
> *Enthusiasm is the vehicle of my life.*

Contemplation of Allah is my companion.

Faith is the source of my power.

Sorrow is my friend.

Knowledge is my weapon.

Patience is my clothing and virtue.

Submission to the Divine Will is my pride.

Truth is my salvation.

Worship is my practice.

And in prayer lies the coolness of my eye

and my peace of mind.

Muhammad's character exemplified a life of love and became a model for all who were called Muslims.

Human history has no greater example of a figure who was both a contemplative and a social revolutionary than Muhammad. On the one hand he devoted himself to meditation, vigils, and fasts; he opened his heart to the Divine and there he heard Gabriel's voice. He listened to the guidance that was given for the various circumstances he encountered; and he transmitted a revelation and a way of life. After that revelation began, he was also commanded to form a community, and eventually a nation, which in an unbelievably short period of time became a unified and dynamic culture. For someone even cursorily acquainted with the facts, it would be difficult to deny that any other single human being has affected so great a number of people so deeply and in so many aspects of their lives. For although Jesus, who is respected and loved by all Muslims, might have influenced a vast number of souls, this influence is diluted by the fact that Christianity comprises a diverse and often contradictory assortment of religious beliefs and includes a very large number of people whose adherence is more nominal than devout, while Islam has remained a relatively unified faith and way of life. The way revealed through Muhammad and the Qur'an enlists from its more than one billion faithful a degree of commitment and energy that the rest of the world finds hard to understand: prayer and ablutions five times a day, a month-long fast, a universal pilgrimage, a single ritual prayer and holy book accepted by all, and a moral framework governing business, social life, the family, and the individual.

In the eyes of Muslims the Prophet's life exemplifies a combination of qualities that include sanctity, wisdom, faith, integrity, strength, justice, generosity, magnanimity, nobility, humanity, and modesty. It was these qualities that shaped the spiritual climate of Islam. Muhammad's speech and actions have been remembered and preserved more exactly than those of perhaps any other historical personality, and in the hearts of Muslims his life became a norm for all of human life.

And yet Muhammad should not be confused with God. He listened to what the Divine revealed even when it criticized his own actions. Muhammad was a human being, not infallible and capable of at least lesser mistakes in thought and speech, yet perfect in this respect: he passed on exactly what was entrusted to him by God. He could do this, at least in part, because he was basically unlettered, a tabula rasa on which God wrote his qualities. He was uncompromisingly truthful and sincere and could transmit the divine message without confusing it with his own ideas. He completely lacked personal ambition or opportunism. In the eyes of Muslims he was a direct instrument of God and he faithfully fulfilled his purpose.

The Prophet came into the world without a father, who had died several months before he was born. His family, Bani Hashim, was one of the most prominent in Mecca, and his grandfather was the undisputed leader of Mecca and caretaker of the Ka'ba and its pilgrims. Shortly after birth, the Prophet was suckled in the desert by a bedouin wet nurse, as was the custom in Mecca, and at the age of two returned to live with his mother, Amina. Four years later, she also died, and the Prophet was taken care of by his grandfather, Abd Al Muttalib. Several years later, Abd Al Muttalib also died, and Muhammad went to live with his uncle Abu Talib. Muhammad knew what it was to be an orphan; he experienced the vulnerability of being dependent on others and he had a lifelong sympathy with orphans and the disadvantaged.

Like his uncle, Abu Talib, the Prophet became a trader, and his success and honesty eventually impressed a wealthy, older widow named Khadija, so much that she asked the twenty-five-year-old Muhammad to marry her—even though she had refused marriage proposals from some of the most prominent men of Mecca. Although she was fifteen years his senior, Muhammad agreed to her proposal. They had a very happy marriage. She bore him four daughters and two sons, although his sons died in early childhood. The Prophet loved her, perhaps more than any other woman in his life. Some years after Khadija died, the Prophet's then wife Aisha narrated: "One day, my jealousy of Khadija got the best of me, and I said to the Prophet that she was nothing more than an old woman and Allah has given you better than her! After [I said] this, the hair on the Prophet's head stood up, and in anger [he] said to me, 'No! By Allah! Allah has not given me better than her! She believed in me when all others disbelieved. She accepted me while all others called me a liar. She spent out of her wealth while all other people deprived me of their wealth. Through her, Allah gave me a child while I was deprived of this from my other wives!'" He held her memory tenderly all through his life, and in later years whenever he would roast a lamb he would even take care to send some of it to Khadija's friends.

The society into which Muhammad was born was lacking in spiritual tradition. They believed vaguely in God, but they also believed that the wood and stone idols they worshipped had a spirit that would intercede with God on their behalf. The Ka'ba was said to have 360 idols placed there as tokens from various Arab tribes, and the Arabs had long abandoned the pure monotheism of Abraham and Ishmael, and their religion had degenerated into superficial customs and superstitions. Muhammad seems to have kept himself aloof from the prevailing customs. In fact, even as a young boy, when someone asked him a question "in the name of Lat and Uzza," two of the goddesses worshipped by the Arabs, Muhammad said he didn't want to be asked anything in their names.

As the Prophet grew older, he became more contemplative. He wondered how there could be so much injustice in the world, how people could merely worship idols of stone and wood instead of the Creator. His deep thought and contemplation led him to spend each lunar month of Ramadan—yes, there was Ramadan at that time, and it had some spiritual significance, although the fast had not yet been instituted—in a cave on Mount Hira not far from the Ka'ba, where he would meditate. At the age of forty, on the twenty-seventh night of the month of Ramadan, his life would be changed forever. The Prophet was meditating in the darkness of the cave, when it was suddenly filled with an intense light. A voice then called to him and said, "Read!" He responded, "I am not able to read." Very few people at that time learned how to read and write, and the Prophet was unlettered. The presence in the cave then grabbed the Prophet and squeezed him so strongly that he could not breathe. It then released him and repeated: "Read!" The Prophet again replied, "I am not able to read." The presence again squeezed the Prophet even more tightly than the first time and repeated the command a third time: "Read!" The Prophet replied for the third time, "I am not able to read." The presence then squeezed the Prophet so tightly that he thought he would die. The presence then told the Prophet, "Read in the name of your Lord who created. [He] created mankind from something that clings. Read! And your Lord is Most Generous. Who taught mankind by the Pen, taught them that which they did not know" (96:1–5). The presence then disappeared, but the Prophet said that those words were "written upon his heart."

Frightened and awed, the Prophet rushed home to his beloved Khadija. Drenched in sweat and trembling, he told her, "Cover me, cover me!" After the Prophet calmed down, he recounted to his wife what he had seen and heard, and he told her that he was afraid he was losing his mind. Khadija answered, "Muhammad, a man like you, who is trustworthy, who cares for his relatives and the less fortunate—a man like you doesn't go crazy!"

She took her husband to her cousin, Waraqah ibn Nawfal, who knew something of the Jewish and Christian scriptures. The Prophet recounted his experience, and Waraqah was astounded, for he understood how the Prophets of Israel had been inspired with divine revelation. In fact, Muhammad's experience seemed to be hinted at by this verse in Deuteronomy: "I will raise them up a Prophet from among their brethren, like unto you, and will put my words in his mouth; and he shall speak unto them all that I shall command him" (Deuteronomy

18:18). But Waraqah had not thought it would be from among the sons of Ishmael because, up until then, every Prophet was from the progeny of Isaac. He told the Prophet, "This is the Great Spirit [the archangel Gabriel] that visited Moses in the past," and he told him that he was the Prophet sent unto his people. Waraqah then lamented his old age and wished he were younger so that he could help the Prophet, but then he added a warning, "For no man has ever brought anything like what you have brought without being opposed and fought by his people, which has always been so. If I live to see that day, I shall stand by you."

Muhammad, who was much respected among the people of Mecca, expressed deep surprise that his people would fight him. He had been known as "Al Amin," the Trustworthy One. Once when the Meccans had decided to rebuild the Ka'ba after it was damaged from a flood, the various tribes fell into dispute over which of them would place the sacred Black Stone in the cornerstone position. The dispute became so intense that they were ready to resort to violence. In order to avert conflict, someone suggested letting the first person to enter the area of the Ka'ba mediate the dispute. When they saw that this person would be none other than Muhammad, they all rejoiced and said, "The Trustworthy One? We're happy with this." Muhammad's solution was that a representative from each of the tribes would hold a corner of a single cloth in which the stone was wrapped and so they could all together set the cornerstone. He successfully mediated their dispute and averted a bloody confrontation among the Meccan tribes.

After the initial revelation, there was an uncomfortable silence for several months. The Prophet longed for the communication to resume. Then, according to the Prophet, "While I was walking along, I heard a voice from heaven and I raised up my eyes, and lo! The Angel that had appeared to me on Hira appeared on the vast horizon between heaven and earth and I was struck with awe and returned home and asked Khadija to enfold me." Then Allah revealed: "O you who are enfolded! Arise and give warning, and magnify your Lord, and purify your clothes, and shun all defilement." This was the second group of verses of the Qur'an (74:1–5) that was revealed to him, and this further confirmed to the Prophet that he was indeed sent by God to the people as his Messenger. After this, verse after verse was revealed over a period of twenty-three years in response to the needs and trials of Muhammad and his community.

The angel would come down to him in various forms, as the Prophet said: "Sometimes it is revealed like the ringing of a bell, and this form of inspiration is the hardest of all. Then this state passes away after I have grasped what is inspired. Sometimes the Angel comes in the form of a man and talks to me and I grasp whatever he says."

Muhammad had no preconceptions or ambitions about assuming authority in his community; in fact he had been a reluctant prophet at first, doubting his own sanity. But gradually, through the ongoing revelations, a mission was revealed to him and his destiny became virtually unavoidable.

The first time he called his people together, the Prophet Muhammad climbed a small mountain called Abi Qubais and gathered everyone to him. He told them, "If I were to tell you that an army was gathered against you behind this mountain, would you believe me?" They all replied in the affirmative: "We have never known you to lie." He then proceeded to tell them of his prophethood and mission. It was his own uncle, Abu Lahab, who stopped the Prophet in his tracks and screamed, "May you perish!" Abu Lahab then dispersed the people and sent them on their way. This was the first inkling of the persecution that the Prophet would face at the hands of the Meccans, and it gives meaning to the words of the Qur'an: "But, for your Lord's sake, be patient and constant!" (74:7). God was preparing the Prophet for the hardship that was to come. In fact, of all the Prophet's enemies, the Prophet's uncle Abu Lahab would be among the harshest.

At first only several members of his family joined this as yet unnamed movement: his wife and four surviving daughters, his young cousin Ali, and his aunt Safiyyah. The most important event at this time, however, was the conversion of his close friend Abu Bakr. Abu Bakr's conversion was extremely important, because it was due to his prominence and influence in the community, as well as his zeal, that those who would subsequently be among the most prominent companions of the Prophet were attracted to the cause.

As the message was spreading among the people of Mecca, the Meccan establishment began to worry deeply. Thus, in order to stem the tide of converts, they resorted to harassment, repression, and even murder. In fact, they murdered the parents of Ammar ibn Yasser, one of the Prophet's Companions, right in front of him and tortured Ammar into maligning the Prophet.

The situation became so dire that the Prophet was extremely concerned about a group of his Companions who were not under the protection of various tribal leaders and whom he himself could not protect. Muhammad had heard of a just Christian king, known as the Negus, across the sea in Abyssinia. Therefore, he recommended that these people, including his own cousin Jafar, should travel there and live under the Negus's protection. When the group presented itself to the king, he wanted to know what sort of religion they practiced. Jafar gave this eloquent testimony to the effect that Muhammad and the revelation had had on their lives:

> O King, we used to live in ignorance and immorality, worshipping idols, eating carrion, committing all kinds of abominations. We did not honor our relatives and we did not help our neighbors. The strong among us exploited the weak. Then God sent us a Prophet, one from among ourselves, whose lineage, integrity, loyalty, and purity were well known to us. He called us to worship God alone and to repudiate all the stones and idols which we and our ancestors used to worship. He commanded us to always speak the truth, to keep our trusts and promises, to help each other, our neighbors, and our relatives, to abstain from blood and other unhealthy things, to avoid fornication, slander, and lies. He commanded us not to take the wealth of orphans, nor to falsely accuse married women. He taught us to worship God alone and not to rely on anything else, to establish daily prayers, to fast, and to offer charity. We trusted him and what he brought from God. Our own people, however, tried to dissuade us and they eventually made life unbearable for us in Mecca, so we chose you and your country in which to live under your protection in justice and peace [from the Prophet's biography (Ibn Hisham)].

The Negus then said, "Would you share with me some of your Prophet's teachings directly?"

And at that Jafar recited a portion of the Surah of Mary: "Mary, therefore, pointed to the child as her only answer. Her people asked, 'How can we inquire of an infant in the cradle?' At this Jesus spoke, 'I am the servant of God to whom He has given the Book and whom He has blessed and commissioned with Prophethood; whom He has enjoined with holding prayer and giving in charity. My mother is innocent and I am neither unjust nor evil. Peace be upon me the day I was born, on the day I shall die, and on the day I shall be resurrected.'"

When the Negus heard these words, he said, "These words must have sprung from the same fountainhead from which the words of our Lord Jesus have sprung." He then drew a line in the sand with his staff and said, "Between your religion and ours is no more difference than the width of this line. You are welcome here."

Not only is this story a clear glimpse into the spiritual world of the first Muslims, it is also evidence of Muhammad's wish to live in harmony with the righteous people of other faiths, and his belief that there is no inherent conflict between the followers of Jesus and the followers of the Qur'an.

Back in Mecca, meanwhile, despite this violent repression, the flow of converts did not cease. In fact, one of the Prophet's most entrenched enemies, Umar ibn Al Khattab, converted to Islam. Umar was such an enemy before his conversion that someone had said, "This donkey of mine will convert before Umar ever does."

He was known as a bit of a bully around town, someone whose wrong side you did not want to be on. He had heard that his sister had joined Muhammad's circle and he was determined to dissuade her from following Muhammad or to kill this charlatan and provocateur himself. He entered a house where his sister had gathered with her husband and a companion of the Prophet. At that moment, the Qur'an was being recited, and something in the sound and meaning of the recitation must have touched Umar's heart. After reading the words, he went straight to Muhammad and joined the fold of Islam. Such was the conversion of the bully Umar, who was destined to become a righteous upholder of justice, the second Caliph after Muhammad.

For the most part, the Prophet was safe from the most severe harassment because his uncle, Abu Talib, vowed to protect him. Yet this protection did not prevent the Meccans from insulting and at times even assaulting the Prophet. Since persecution did not work, the Meccans eventually imposed a form of economic sanction on the Prophet, his followers, and his entire tribe, the Bani Hashim, preventing others from trading or intermarrying with them. Furthermore, they were expelled from their homes and forced to live in hunger among the mountains surrounding Mecca. This sanctions regime continued for three years until some of the nobles of Mecca refused to go along with this cruel treatment of their kinsmen. This period was very difficult for the Prophet. As a result of the boycott, his wife Khadija, his most important source of support and comfort, died. Soon after her death, his uncle Abu Talib, his only source of protection, also died. With the death of Abu Talib, the persecution of the Meccans increased substantially. It was becoming more and more dangerous for the Prophet in Mecca. Seeing that there was little hope for his people to live in peace in Mecca, the Prophet went north to the town of Taif to share his message, but the people there violently rejected it and sent the street children after him to expel him from the city, stoning and badly bloodying his feet. This was one of the lowest points for the Prophet. After he left the city limits of Taif, he sought refuge in an orchard and addressed this prayer to God:

> To You I complain of my weakness, resourcelessness and humiliation before the people. You are the Most Merciful, the Lord of the weak and my Master. To whom will you confide me? To one estranged, bearing ill will, or an enemy given power over me? If Your wrath is not upon me, I care not, for Your favor is abundant upon me. I seek refuge in the light of Your countenance by which all darkness is dispelled and every affair of this world and the next is set right, lest Your anger should descend upon me or Your displeasure light upon me. I need only your pleasure and satisfaction for only You enable me to do good and evade the evil. There is no power and no might save in you.

This year was called "The Year of Sadness," and it was in this year that a great spiritual gift was bestowed on Muhammad—the famous night journey and ascent.

This night journey is mentioned in the Qur'an: "Glory be to the One Who did take His servant for a Journey by night from the Sacred Mosque [in Mecca] to the farthest Mosque [in Jerusalem], whose precincts We did bless, in order that We might show him some of Our Signs: for He is the One Who is All-Hearing and All-Seeing" (17:1).

The event is described in this way: Upon arriving in Jerusalem, the Prophet led a ritual prayer in which many of the other prophets also prayed. He then ascended through the "seven heavens," meeting various prophets—Moses, Jesus,

Abraham, Aaron, Joseph—along the way. The pinnacle of this journey was the Prophet's entering the intimate presence of the Divine, which is mystically described as coming within "two bow-lengths or nearer." It was here that God ordained the five daily prayers that would become the basic practice of Muslims from then on. It is said that the prescribed daily prayers were originally fifty in number, but Muhammad met Moses on the way back, and Moses, experienced prophet that he was, pleaded with Muhammad to ask God for a reduction, knowing full well how weak we humans are. In response to the repeated exhortations of Moses, the Prophet eventually had the number of prayers reduced to five, but with a promise from God that Muhammad's people would receive all the benefit of fifty prayers.

This miraculous night journey served to comfort the Prophet and strengthen his resolve to continue proclaiming the message of Islam. The next morning, the Prophet told everyone of his night journey, but his story drew ridicule. Even some believers doubted his story, and some even left Islam because of it. At that time, the trip to Jerusalem took one month each way. To claim that he went to Jerusalem, then heaven, and then back to Mecca in a fortnight was sheer madness. On the other hand, some view this as one of the many proofs of Muhammad's sincerity and prophethood. Who in their right mind, trying hard to convince people, would tell such an implausible story if it were not the truth?

Why would the Prophet purposely subject himself to ridicule? The Meccans, seeking to discredit the Prophet, asked him to describe the Holy City in Jerusalem in detail. He was able to answer every one of their questions because, according to the Prophet, God placed the city before his eyes at that time.

In addition, the Prophet told them that in three days a certain caravan would be arriving from the direction of Jerusalem, and he told the Meccans to ask the caravan a number of specific questions. They did so, and everything the Prophet said about the caravan was confirmed. Still, despite this, most of the Meccans refused to believe.

The situation seemed desperate for the Prophet at this point, but respite was soon to come. A small contingent from the city of Yathrib, two hundred miles to the north of Mecca, heard of the Prophet's teaching. He secretly took an oath of loyalty from them, and he sent one of his Companions to teach the inhabitants of Yathrib about Islam. Within one year, many in the city of Yathrib had accepted Islam, and they invited the Prophet to live there. He took another oath of loyalty from the inhabitants of Yathrib, and he then asked every believer in Mecca to migrate there. The Prophet stayed behind until everyone had left Mecca safely, and then he and his dear companion Abu Bakr received permission from God to emigrate. Yathrib was then renamed Medina, meaning "the City of the Prophet." This is the major turning point in the history of Islam. Medina was the first Islamic city-state, and the Prophet was its spiritual and political leader. This emigration, or *hijrah*, is the start of the Islamic calendar.

When he arrived in Medina, Muhammad forged an alliance with the various tribes, even though not all of them accepted him as a prophet. This alliance was codified in the Constitution of Medina, one of the first constitutions—if not the first—in human history.

To quote the biographer Maxime Rodinson, "Muhammad came as an arbiter, without assuming the power of a chief of state . . . [He] acted as a Bedouin sayyid [chief], . . . deriving his power entirely from his moral ascendancy. He treated his disciples as his equals, with courtesy and respect."

This was a disaster for the Meccans. Not only had they failed to stem the tide of Islam, but now the Prophet would have a base of operations from which he would gain strength and attract more people to the faith.

The Muslims who had emigrated to Medina were generously taken in by the Ansar, or "helpers," of Medina, as they came to be called, but their economic situation was dire. The Muslims had lost all that they owned when they were forced to leave Mecca. It was at this time that Muhammad made a controversial, strategic decision to attack a Meccan caravan.

The Prophet and his people had been unjustly exiled to Medina because the Meccans expelled him, just as the Qur'an says: "And how many cities, with more power than your city which has driven you out, have We destroyed [for their sins]? And none there were to aid them" (47:13). In addition, the Prophet remarked about Mecca: "What a beautiful city you are and how ardently I love you. Had my people not exiled me, I would have never settled anywhere else." This expulsion, therefore, was itself an act of great injustice. Thus the Prophet attacked the Meccan caravan to recoup this lost wealth. Furthermore, the Prophet engaged in offensive fighting in order to make a show of force and discourage other tribes from attacking the nascent Islamic community.

Why did the Meccans fight the Prophet so viciously? It was not, as some have claimed, simply because he challenged their idols. It was truly the Prophet's message that was threatening to their way of life, the status quo. Although the Meccans were pagans, worshipping other gods besides the One God of Abraham, they still believed in and worshipped that One God.

These lesser gods were intermediaries that "brought them nearer" to God. In addition, they kept some of the traditions of Abraham, such as the annual pilgrimage to Mecca, alive, although it had been corrupted by superstitions and commercialism, for the Meccans profited handsomely from the pilgrimage. They made up rules for the pilgrimage; for example, pilgrims could only circumambulate the Ka'ba in clothes sold by the Meccans. If pilgrims could not afford to buy the clothing, they would have to circumambulate naked. If Muhammad succeeded in abolishing these practices, their monopoly on the pilgrimage trade would be destroyed, and thus the message of Islam had to be stopped. In addition, the very phrase "There is nothing worthy of worship except God" necessarily meant that they must submit their will to that of God, and this, as well, was difficult to accept. They could not continue ignoring the plight of the poor. They could not continue to take advantage of those who did not have a strong tribal affiliation. They could not accept that the will of God might not always be in keeping with their agenda. That is why they fought the Prophet. In fact, this is why all the prophets of old were opposed by their people. The agenda of God is frequently at odds with the vested interests of those in power.

There were some early skirmishes with the Meccans, and in one of these, the Muslims attacked and killed a Meccan by the name of Amr ibn Al Hadrami during one of the sacred months in which fighting was supposedly prohibited. The Muslims did not realize that they were fighting in a sacred month when the skirmish took place. Nevertheless, this was an enormous scandal, and the Meccans leveled the charge that "Muhammad no longer keeps the sacred months sacred." The Prophet, for his part, refused to take any of the spoils from this expedition because it was undertaken during a sacred month. In addition, God revealed to the Prophet this verse from the Qur'an: "They question you [O Muhammad] with regard to warfare in the sacred month. Say: warfare therein is a great transgression, but to turn people from the way of God, and to expel them thence, is a greater sin with God; for persecution is worse than killing" (2:217). This verse did not condone the attack on the Meccans during the sacred month. Yet it reminded the Meccans that they had committed an even greater sin by their previous actions against the Prophet and his community.

These skirmishes eventually led to the first major battle between the Muslims and the Meccans: the Battle of Badr. The Muslims were outnumbered three to one: the Meccans had an army of one thousand and the Muslims numbered only three hundred. Yet despite their small number, the Muslims decisively defeated the Meccans in just a few hours. This was a major blow for the Meccans, and the Battle of Badr claimed the lives of many of the harshest enemies of the Prophet.

The bitter defeat of the Meccans at Badr led them to regroup and gather an army of three thousand. This time, the battle was fought at the mountain of Uhud. The Muslims had initially defeated the Meccans here as well, but a portion of the Muslim army disobeyed a direct order of the Prophet, and this gave the Meccans a temporary advantage. They capitalized on this advantage to attack the Prophet directly, and they severely wounded him. The Muslims fled up the mountain of Uhud, escaping the Meccan swords, and the battle was ended. It is important to note here that, although the Prophet's Companions disobeyed a direct order, resulting in his almost being killed, the Prophet did not punish those Companions. The Qur'an talks about this: "It is part of the Mercy of God that you deal gently with them. Were you severe or harsh-hearted, they would have broken away from you: so pass over their faults, and ask for forgiveness for them; and consult them in affairs. Then, when you have taken a decision, put your trust in God. For God loves those who put their trust in Him" (3:159).

Although the Meccans had "won" the second half of the battle, it was really a truce, because the Meccans did not achieve any of their goals: the Muslims were not destroyed; the Prophet was not killed. In a short while the Meccans would gather the biggest army ever assembled in the history of the Arabs, ten thousand men, to finally destroy Islam and the Muslim community at Medina. The Prophet decided to stay in Medina and defend the city directly, building a large trench around the city for protection. Despite the forty-day siege of the city, the Meccans failed and were defeated.

A year after this Battle of the Trench, the Muslims and the Meccans signed a ten-year truce, the Treaty of Hudaybiyah. After only two years, however, a tribe allied with the Meccans broke the treaty. Muhammad quickly assembled an army and set out toward Mecca, gathering more troops from various tribes along the way until eventually there were ten thousand soldiers. With the army camped a few miles away from the town, Abu Sufyan, one of the Meccan leaders, spied the Muslim army and through a chance meeting with one of Muhammad's commanders was brought into the camp to consult with Muhammad. Abu Sufyan was treated well by Muhammad and an amnesty was offered to all Meccans who did not oppose the arrival of the army. It was Muhammad's wish to preserve the sanctity of Mecca from unnecessary bloodshed.

Muhammad entered the city with hardly a drop of blood

shed, and he gave his former enemies a general amnesty. Thus the final conquest of Mecca was a moral, not a military, victory.

After the conquest of Mecca, within a few years the whole of the Arabian Peninsula had come under Muslim rule. In the year 631, the Prophet performed his farewell pilgrimage to Mecca, where he gave his final instructions to the Muslim faithful. In the year 632, the Prophet died in Medina at the age of sixty-three. These are Muhammad's final instructions to his community:

> O people, listen well to my words, for I do not know whether I shall meet you again on such an occasion in the future. O people, your lives and your property shall be inviolate until you meet your Sustainer. The safety of your lives and of your property shall be as inviolate as this holy day and holy month. Remember that you will indeed meet your Sustainer, and that He will indeed reckon your deeds. Thus do I warn you. Whoever of you is keeping a trust of someone else shall return that trust to its rightful owner. All interest obligation shall henceforth be waived. Your capital, however, is yours to keep. You will neither inflict nor suffer inequity. God has judged that there shall be no interest and that all the interest due to 'Abbas ibn 'Abd al Muttalib shall henceforth be waived. Every right of retribution arising out of homicide in pre-Islamic days is henceforth waived. And the first such right that I waive is that arising from the murder of Rabi'ah ibn al Harith ibn 'Abd al Muttalib. O people, the devil has lost all hope of ever being worshipped in this land of yours. Neverthe-less, he still is anxious to determine the lesser of your

deeds. Beware of him, therefore, for the safety of your religion. O people, intercalation or tampering with the calendar is evidence of great misbelief and confirms the
deniers in their misguidance. They indulge in it one year
and forbid it the next in order to make permissible that
which God forbade, and to forbid that which God has
made permissible. The pattern according to which the
time is reckoned is always the same. With God, the
months are twelve in number. Four of them are holy.
Three of these are successive and one occurs singly between the months of Jumada and Sha'ban. O people, to
you a right belongs with respect to your women and to
your women a right with respect to you. It is your right
that they not mix with anyone of whom you do not ap-
prove, as well as never to commit adultery. But if they do,
then God has permitted you to isolate them within their
homes and to chastise them without cruelty. But if they
abide by your right, then to them belongs the right to be
fed and clothed in kindness. Do treat your women well
and be kind to them, for they are your partners and committed helpers. Remember that you have taken them as
your wives and enjoyed their flesh only under God's trust
and with His permission. Reason well, therefore, my people, and ponder these words which I now convey to you.
I am leaving you with the Book of God and the Sunnah
of His Prophet. If you follow them, you will never go
astray. O people, listen well to my words. Learn that
every Muslim is a brother to every Muslim and that the
Muslims constitute one family. Nothing shall be legitimate to a Muslim which belongs to a fellow Muslim unless it was given freely and willingly. Do not, therefore, do

injustice to your own selves. O God, have I conveyed
Your message?

This is a basic overview of the Prophet's life; a more exhaustive
study of the Prophet's biography is beyond the scope of this
book. We refer the reader to the sources listed in Appendix I
for further reading and study. The Prophet Muhammad, more
than any other religious figure in history, has had his reputation
repeatedly and systematically attacked and maligned. In addition, his history has been systematically distorted to further his
negative image, especially in the West. This began during the
time of the Crusades, and has been relentless ever since, and a
clarification of these incidents in his life is in order now. One
of the most common assertions made about the Prophet is that
he was a bloodthirsty religious imposter who murdered anyone
who did not follow his "made-up" religion. These accusers cite
as evidence several incidents in Medina, especially those having to do with the Jewish tribes of Medina. What these people
do is distort the full story of these incidents in order to paint
the Prophet in a negative light, and they do not explain the circumstances surrounding these incidents.

The city of Medina, called Yathrib before the Prophet's migration, was primarily composed of three main groups: the
tribe of Aws, the tribe of Khazraj, and several Jewish tribes.
Both the Aws and Khazraj were pagans, and they had a long-
standing and bitter rivalry. In addition, several different Jewish
tribes were allied to each pagan tribe. No one group was able to
dominate over the other two. The migration of the Muslims
from Mecca and of the Prophet to be their ruler added a further dimension to the social dynamics of the city. Contrary to
some assertions, most of the Aws and Khazraj accepted Islam

and accepted the Prophet as their spiritual and political leader. The Jewish tribes, on the whole, rejected the prophethood of Muhammad, with a few exceptions. There did remain a very small number of pagans in Medina after the Prophet settled there, and some of these, in fact, feigned acceptance of Islam but secretly worked for the destruction of the nascent Islamic state. These were known as the Hypocrites, and this is what they are called in Islamic history and in the Qur'an.

When the Prophet came to Medina, one of the first things he did was draw up an agreement and alliance with the Aws, the Khazraj, and the Jewish tribes of Medina. All were included in the new city-state, and the Prophet mandated that Jewish law govern the Jews, with him as head of state. Despite this alliance, however, there were several skirmishes with various Jewish tribes, and as a result, most of the Jews were killed or expelled, or they emigrated from Medina. The Prophet's detractors say this is evidence of the Prophet's "bloodthirstiness." This could not be further from the truth. First of all, the Prophet called the Jews to Islam almost immediately after he arrived in Medina, and they refused. Despite this, however, he formed an alliance with them. If the Prophet was a "bloodthirsty killer," as they say, it would make sense that he would immediately attack them and either kill or expel them from Medina. He did not do so, however, and he included them in the new Medinan constitution, with full rights of citizenship. Nevertheless, he did fight with some of the Jews in Medina. The Prophet's critics, however, do not explain the circumstances and simply state: "The Prophet attacked such and such a Jewish tribe" and stop at that. This is grossly misleading and deceitful.

The first of these skirmishes occurred soon after the Prophet arrived in Medina. One of the Jewish tribes, Bani Qaynuqa, was made up of gold merchants. A Muslim woman was shopping in their marketplace when some of the Jews of Bani Qaynuqa asked her to show her face, and she refused. She later sat down and leaned against a tree trunk, and one of the Bani Qaynuqa tied the edges of her clothing—unbeknownst to her—to the tree trunk. When she got up, her clothes stayed behind her and she was exposed. The group of men behind this prank then began to laugh. Another Muslim at the market fought with the man who tied the woman's clothes to the tree trunk and ended up killing him. A group of Bani Qaynuqa then fought that Muslim man and killed him. This series of events was a clear breach of the alliance between the Muslims and Bani Qaynuqa. When the Prophet learned what happened, he laid siege to the tribe of Bani Qaynuqa. They initially resolved to fight, but they later lost their resolve and agreed to submit to the Prophet's verdict. Before the Prophet could mete out his decision, a man named Abdullah bin Ubay, the leader of the Hypocrites in Medina, went to the Prophet and demanded, "Treat my confederates kindly." The Bani Qaynuqa were his allies before the Prophet came to Medina. The Prophet initially ignored him. Abdullah ibn Ubay persisted, and he even grabbed the Prophet's armor and refused to let go, repeating, "Treat my confederates kindly!" The Prophet then said, "They are yours." Abdullah bin Ubay then decreed that the Bani Qaynuqa should leave Medina, and they obeyed. Those who seek to malign the Prophet claim that the Prophet exiled the Bani Qaynuqa for no reason, failing to mention the incident surrounding their departure. Furthermore, even though Abdullah bin Ubay had publicly declared himself a Muslim, the Prophet did not punish him for his act of treason against the state. This further debunks the myth that the Prophet was a "bloodthirsty killer."

A very similar situation occurred with another Jewish tribe, Bani Nadir, four years after the Prophet migrated to Medina. Some of the Arab tribes surrounding Medina had sent delegations to the Prophet declaring that their tribes had accepted Islam, and they requested that the Prophet send them some of his companions as teachers to spread Islam to the rest of the tribes. The Prophet happily obliged. These tribes, however, were lying to the Prophet. Once the delegations left Medina with the Muslim ambassadors, they treacherously murdered them in cold blood. This happened on more than one occasion. One of those Muslims who was attacked survived, and he later mistakenly killed two people from the tribe of Bani Amir in revenge for this act of treachery. Since Bani Amir had a nonaggression treaty with Muhammad, the Prophet decided to pay blood money to Bani Amir for this act of murder, and in Arab society at that time, this payment settled the dispute. Since the Jewish tribe of Bani Nadir were allies of Bani Amir, the Prophet requested that Bani Nadir contribute to the blood money payment, and they agreed to help pay the blood money. Bani Nadir lived some distance away from the city center of Medina, so the Prophet waited for Bani Nadir to gather the money while waiting outside the wall of their citadel.

The leaders of Bani Nadir then paused and talked among themselves. "You will never find Muhammad in a similar manner," they said. The Prophet had come with only three Companions, relatively unguarded from harm. He usually was heavily guarded by his Companions, because there were numerous assassination attempts against him. The leaders of Bani

Nadir continued, "So who will climb atop this house and throw a stone on him (Muhammad) and relieve us of him?" One of them volunteered. As this impromptu assassination plot was being hatched, the Prophet simply got up from where he was sitting and left, leaving his Companions behind. His Companions thought he went to answer the call of nature, but when he did not return after a while, they became worried as to his whereabouts. They returned to Medina to find that the Prophet was gathering to fight Bani Nadir. The archangel Gabriel had informed the Prophet of Bani Nadir's plan to kill him—again, a clear violation of the alliance he made with them. The Prophet gathered an army and laid siege to Bani Nadir. They fortified their positions and stayed put in their citadel. Abdullah ibn Ubay, even though he had declared his faith in Islam, secretly sent word to Bani Nadir that he and his group would help them in their fight with the Prophet, and this emboldened their resolve. This was a lie, and Abdullah ibn Ubay never sent his help. Bani Nadir lost their will to fight, and they asked the Prophet to spare their lives in return for their leaving Medina with everything their camels could carry except their weapons. The Prophet agreed to these terms, and Bani Nadir left Medina peacefully. Again, if the Prophet hated Jews and wanted nothing else but to kill them, he would have refused their offer. He did not.

A much more serious incident occurred with a third Jewish tribe, Bani Quraiza, and this time blood was spilled. There is a context to this incident as well, and it was not, as some claim, due to the Prophet's war on anyone who did not believe in Islam. In the Battle of the Trench, when the Meccans laid siege to Medina with an army ten thousand strong, the city was well fortified from the east, west, and south. The north side of Medina, however, was vulnerable to attack. The Meccans would be coming from the south, and the Prophet used every man he had to protect the front of the city from attack. To fully protect Medina, he sent word to Bani Quraiza, a Jewish tribe that lived in the north end of the city, reaffirming their alliance with the Muslims and making sure that they would protect the rear of Medina from attack. Bani Quraiza agreed and reaffirmed their alliance with the Prophet. The Meccan army came, and the trench was a formidable defense. The Meccans tried unsuccessfully to breach Medina's defenses for several days. The Meccans then tried to exploit the weakness of the city in the north by convincing Bani Quraiza to break their alliance with the Prophet and attack the Muslims from the rear. When the Muslims learned of this plot, most of the one thousand Muslims who were defending the city from a frontal attack abandoned the Prophet to protect their own homes. The plan fell through, but there was a very real possibility that the Muslim community would have been wiped out because Bani Quraiza broke the treaty. The Meccans abandoned their siege of Medina after forty days, and the Prophet then immediately laid siege to Bani Quraiza, because they broke their treaty with him.

Once again, Bani Quraiza initially resolved to fight, but eventually under siege they soon lost this resolve and agreed to submit to whatever punishment the Prophet deemed appropriate. At this point, some of the Prophet's Companions, true believers and not Hypocrites, made a request: "Treat our confederates kindly, just as you treated the confederates of the Khazraj tribe kindly." Bani Quraiza, it turned out, were the allies of the Aws tribe, while Bani Qaynuqa were allies of Abdullah ibn Ubay, who was of the rival Khazraj tribe. Old tribal rivalries were supposed to have been abolished by the unity of Islam, but old habits died hard, especially in seventh-century Arabia. The Prophet then asked if the Aws would agree to have their leader, Sa'ad ibn Mu'ath, render the proper punishment for Bani Quraiza. The Aws enthusiastically agreed. It was Sa'ad who decided that all the men should be killed, and the women and children placed in servitude. This was as a result of the betrayal by Bani Quraiza at a time of war—high treason against the state. Even in the United States, the punishment for treason is death. In addition, during the reprisal against Bani Quraiza, one member of the tribe came to the Prophet and told him, "I swear by God, when the Jews decided to betray you, I was the only one who refused to go along." The Prophet let him go free. Had the Prophet been "bloodthirsty," he would have called this person a liar and had him killed. He did not.

Another common distortion of the Prophet's biography is the claim that he signed the Treaty of Hudaibiyah at a time of weakness as a ruse only to break it two years later and attack an unsuspecting Mecca. This also could not be further from the truth. In the sixth year after the Prophet migrated to Medina, he decided he wanted to make a lesser pilgrimage, or *umrah*, to the holy house at Mecca. This consists of circumambulating the Ka'ba seven times and running between the mountains of Safa and Marwa, just like during the Hajj. Afterward, an animal is sacrificed for the sake of God, and its meat distributed among the poor. The Prophet gathered 1,200 of his followers, all dressed in *ihram* garb, clearly indicating that they intended to make the lesser pilgrimage and not fight. Yet, the Prophet was not foolhardy; he had his weapons with him on a separate camel in the caravan, in case the Meccans or anyone else attacked them. He set out with the Muslims toward Mecca, and he took them completely by surprise. They sent an army to prevent him from entering the Holy Precincts, a large area surrounding the Ka'ba itself. Once he entered the Holy Precincts, they could not fight him there, as ordained by God. The Prophet, for his part, encamped just short of the border of the Holy Precincts, and thus the Meccans were unclear about his intentions. The Meccans sent several delegations to ask the Prophet what he intended, and each time he told them that he wanted to make the lesser pilgrimage. The Meccans refused, and this made them look very bad in the eyes of the Arabs. Although they were the caretakers of the Ka'ba, they could not prevent anyone, even their archenemy Muhammad, from performing a lesser pilgrimage to God's house. To solve this awkward and distressing problem, the Meccans decided to form a nonaggression treaty—the famous Treaty of Hudaybiyah—with the Prophet. The Prophet agreed.

The Meccans stipulated the following to the Prophet: 1) he could not make the lesser pilgrimage this year but could return for three days, and three days only, the following year; 2) there would be a general truce for ten years, and each party would be safe from the other's swords; 3) if anyone from Mecca escaped to join the Muslims in Medina, the Prophet would have to return him to the Meccans; 4) however, if a Muslim from Medina wished to leave the Prophet and come to Mecca, the Meccans did not have to return that person to Medina; and 5) any other tribe that was allied with either party in the treaty was subject to the terms of the treaty. While the terms were being dictated, representatives of the tribe of Bani Bakr were

present, and they declared that they were allied with the Meccans. In addition, representatives from the tribe of Khuza-ah,
the archenemies of Bani Bakr, declared that they were allied
with the Prophet. The Muslims, when they heard of the terms
of the treaty to which the Prophet had agreed, became very upset. In fact, for the first time, they disobeyed a direct order of
the Prophet to shave their heads (indicating that the lesser pilgrimage had been completed). On the surface, the terms of the
treaty were very lopsided in the Meccans' favor, but the
Prophet knew God would not abandon him. The most important thing for the Prophet was the ten years of peace that the
treaty would herald.

Less than two years into the treaty, the tribe of Bani Bakr
treacherously attacked Khuza-ah, in clear violation of the terms
of the Treaty of Hudaybiyah. Not only that, these members of
Khuza-ah were murdered within the Holy Precincts, where
fighting—even among archrivals—is strictly forbidden, and
they were aided by some of the Meccans. The Meccans knew
that the Prophet would march on Mecca in retaliation for this
treachery, and thus they tried to renegotiate the terms of the
treaty before—they hoped—the Prophet would learn of what
Bani Bakr did. The leader of the Meccans himself, Abu Sufyan,
went to Medina to talk to the Prophet, but it was already too
late. The Prophet gathered ten thousand soldiers to march on
Mecca, the largest army in the history of Islam. When he entered the city, he granted amnesty to anyone who stayed within
their homes. In addition, after Mecca was clearly conquered,
the Prophet forgave the Meccans despite all that they had done
in the past. The conquest of Mecca was perhaps the most
bloodless of religious conquests in history, with only a few peo-

ple being killed. The Meccans were terrified that the Prophet would exact brutal retribution; he did not.

Those who wish to slander the Prophet claim that he only agreed to this treaty because he was weak, and he used the treaty to gather the necessary strength to attack the unsuspecting Meccans two years later. This is clearly not true. First of all, if anything, the Prophet was in a position of strength: he had just defeated the Meccans when they gathered their army of ten thousand to attack Medina, and the Prophet also attacked and defeated those tribes that joined in this campaign. The fact that the Meccans wanted to enter into a treaty with the Prophet showed that they did not wish to fight the Prophet, fearing another defeat at his hands. Had the Prophet been truly "weak," as his critics insist, the Meccans would have attacked and killed him at that time, especially since he had encamped outside the boundaries of the Holy Precincts. Secondly, the terms of the treaty were completely lopsided in the Meccans' favor as noted above, yet the Prophet still agreed to the terms, despite strong and bitter opposition in his own camp to even signing a treaty with the Meccans. Finally, the history of the Prophet clearly shows that it was the Meccans, not the Prophet, who broke the treaty. Had the Meccans stayed true to the terms of the treaty they imposed on the Prophet, he would not have marched on Mecca.

Muslims believe that the Prophet Muhammad (peace be upon him) is the last of the prophets. Indeed, he is called the Seal of the Prophets, like the wax seal on an envelope. Yet, the Prophet Muhammad was more than just a prophet, he was also a messenger of God, because he brought with him a message from God, a holy scripture. That scripture, that message, is the Qur'an, and it is the lasting miracle of the Prophet Muhammad. It is the most important text for Muslims, and it is the source of all that is Islam. It is also, unfortunately, just as misunderstood as the religion of Islam itself, and—just like its deliverer—the Qur'an has been slandered, attacked, and maligned, especially after the horrific attacks of September 11.

4

The Qur'an

The Message of Muhammad

Read in the name of your Lord who created; created mankind from a germ cell [or something which clings]; Read, and your Lord is most Generous; the One who taught by the Pen; taught the human being what it did not know.

With these words, what Muslims believe is the final revelation from God began to descend to the earth. These were the first verses of the Qur'an revealed by the archangel Gabriel to the Prophet Muhammad in the cave of Mount Hira in 610 c.e. For the next twenty-three years, Muhammad would receive intermittent revelations in response to his circumstances and needs and those of his community. He received the final words only nine days before his death.

The Qur'an, which means "recitation" in Arabic, is our holy scripture, our source of law, inspiration, guidance, and spiritual comfort. Composed of 114 chapters, (or Surahs), the Qur'an has more than six thousand verses.

The Qur'an should be approached and judged on its own terms.

> This book, no doubt, is a source of guidance for those who are mindful of God. (2:2)

> It is He who sent down to you in truth the Book, confirming what went before it. He sent down the Law [of Moses] and the Gospel before this as a guide to mankind. And now He has revealed the Criterion. (Surah Al-Imran: 3)

> Will they not, then, try to understand this Qur'an? Had it issued from any but God, they would surely have found in it many inner contradictions. (Nisaa: 82)

> And if you doubt any part of what We have bestowed from on high, step by step, upon Our servant, then produce a surah of similar merit, and call upon any other than God to bear witness for you—if what you say is true. (2:23)

As the selections above suggest, the Qur'an makes certain claims: It is a book without internal contradictions. It is from the same source as previous revelations, including those of Moses and Jesus. Finally, for those who can hear it and understand it in Arabic, the tongue of its revelation, the Qur'an is expressed in a language of unsurpassed depth and beauty. The Qur'an is the lasting legacy of the Prophet's mission, and his greatest miracle. To fully discuss the Qur'an would take volumes; indeed, it has occupied some of the greatest minds for a

lifetime. In this chapter, we will get only a taste, a hint of the
Qur'an and its significance for Muslims. We again refer the
reader to the sources listed in Appendix I for more information.

The chapters are arranged more or less in order of decreasing length, an arrangement that was specified by the Prophet
himself. The Qur'anic chapters can also be divided into two
categories, the ones revealed when the Prophet was living in
Mecca, and those revealed when he lived in Medina. In many
copies of the Qur'an, the beginning of the chapters will list
whether the chapter was revealed in Mecca or Medina. This
distinction is not trivial, because the theme, style, and content
of the Meccan chapters differ significantly from those of Medinan origin.

The chapters revealed in Mecca are more lyrical and universal, while the chapters revealed in Medina are typically longer
than those revealed in Mecca, and they begin to include the
guidance needed for a community, outlining the rules for divorce, inheritance, dietary restrictions, relations with other religions, and so forth. These chapters, for instance, discuss
relations with the "People of the Book," i.e., Jews and Christians, and contain stories about Jesus and Mary.

The original text of the Qur'an has been preserved over the
fourteen centuries since the Prophet's mission and has not been
altered in any way. From the earliest times, the verses of the
Qur'an were memorized by members of the community and
their accuracy fastidiously guarded. While it is true that the
complete method of Arabic transcription was not in use from
the beginning and some elements of the pronunciation were
not necessarily indicated in the first written versions, the oral
tradition had its own standards of verification that were at least

as strict as any written tradition. Muslims believe this is one of the miraculous qualities of the Qur'an and a fulfillment of this verse: "Verily We have sent down the Message, and we will assuredly preserve it" (15:9).

If you pick up a copy of the Qur'an and read it from cover to cover with the expectation of finding a linear and thematic text, arranged according to specific subjects, you may be bewildered by the seemingly random and repetitive arrangement of its content. The beauty and significance of its order does not reveal itself immediately to the linear, conceptual mind, but the Qur'an isn't necessarily meant to be a linear narrative. It was revealed in stages over more than two decades. This is why the study of the Prophet's biography is so important to the study of the Qur'an. In addition, the gradual revelation of the Qur'an explains how some verses seem to contradict each other. For example, it is well known that Islam prohibits the consumption of alcohol and other intoxicants, as clearly outlined in this verse: "O you who believe! Intoxicants, gambling, [dedication of] stones, and [divination by] arrows are an abomination of Satan's handiwork; therefore, eschew them that you may prosper" (5:90). Thus, it would seem odd that this verse would also be in the Qur'an: "O you who believe! Do not approach the prayers with a mind befogged [i.e., intoxicated] until you understand all that you say" (4:43). In addition, this verse makes even less sense: "They ask you concerning wine and gambling. Say: 'In them is great sin, and some profit, for men; but the sin is greater than the profit'" (2:219). Taken together, these verses seem contradictory. When one takes the revelation process of the Qur'an into account, however, the verses make complete sense. Islam evolved over time and the Qur'an reflects the changing circumstances of Muhammad and his community and their own readiness to embrace and enact the guidance being offered. The harsh and barbaric society in which the Prophet lived had entrenched norms that could not be instantly eradicated. The first priority for the Prophet was to firmly establish the centrality of God in the hearts of the people. That's why so many verses of the Qur'an revealed in Mecca dealt with this concept. This was more important, in the beginning of Islam, than the prohibition of alcohol. In addition, consumption of alcohol was very entrenched in Arab society. For the Prophet to say, "Your worship of these idols is falsehood" was a big enough change for the Arabs. If he had said, "Abandon your gods, and, by the way, stop drinking alcohol," there would have been a revolt. Thus, prohibition of alcohol came in stages.

The first hint of alcohol's eventual prohibition came in verse 2:219. "They ask you concerning wine and gambling. Say: 'In them is great sin, and some profit, for men; but the sin is greater than the profit.'" In fact, some of the Companions of the Prophet, upon learning this verse, knew that God would eventually ban alcohol, even though the text did not say so explicitly. Later, as the new Muslim converts' faith in Islam grew stronger, God said not to pray when drunk (4:43). If one has to pray five times a day, drinking alcohol is pretty difficult. Finally, when the Muslims were ready, the final prohibition came (5:90). In fact, when this verse was revealed, it was said that so much wine was discarded that it flowed like rivers in the streets of Medina.

Muslims believe the Prophet received revelation from God just as previous prophets did. "We have sent you inspiration, as We sent it to Noah and the Messengers after him: we sent inspiration to Abraham, Ishmael, Isaac, Jacob and the Tribes, to Jesus, Job, Jonah, Aaron, and Solomon, and to David We gave the Psalms. Of some prophets We have already told you the story; of others We have not;—and to Moses God spoke directly" (4:163–164).

At one point, someone asked Muhammad how the divine inspiration was revealed to him. He replied, "Sometimes, it is revealed like the ringing of a bell; this form of inspiration is the hardest of all, and then this state passes off after I have grasped what is inspired. Sometimes the Angel comes in the form of a man and talks to me, and I grasp whatever he says." Some verses were revealed in response to a specific incident, such as the verses defending the Prophet's wife from accusations of adultery (24:11–20). Others were revealed to guide the believers on a certain issue, such as this verse: "Nor come nigh to adultery: for it is a shameful deed and an evil, opening the road [to other evils]" (17:32). Still others are a direct response to a challenge or question posed to the Prophet: "They ask you [O Muhammad] what they should spend [in charity]. Say: 'Whatever you spend that is good, is for parents and kindred and orphans and those in want and for wayfarers. And whatever you do that is good, God knows it well' " (2:215). Some verses were revealed to comfort and strengthen the Prophet: "Nun. By the Pen and that which is written. You are not, by the Grace of your Lord, mad or possessed. Nay, verily for you is a Reward unfailing, and you stand upon an exalted standard of character" (68:1–4). A great deal of the Qur'an discusses the prophets of old. In fact, the Qur'an mentions Moses and Jesus by name more times than the Prophet Muhammad himself. In addition, there is a chapter called "Mary," named after the mother of Jesus Christ.

THE AUTHORSHIP OF THE QUR'AN

A common misunderstanding is that the Prophet is the "author" of the Qur'an. As eloquent as Muhammad could be in his pithy and wise counsels to his people, the language of Muhammad is not the language of the Qur'an. It should be kept in mind that Muhammad experienced the revelation of the Qur'an as a complete revelation in a language of inimitable beauty. It was well known among all the Meccans that the Prophet was unlettered; he could neither read nor write. Furthermore, he was not even versed in poetry, which was much loved by the Arabs. Yet, the language of the Qur'an was so eloquent that it surpassed the language of even the best Arab poets. The Qur'an itself challenged the Arabs at the time of the Prophet to come up with one chapter equal to the Qur'an, but they could not. This is part of the miracle of the Qur'an.

Furthermore, there are a number of verses that instruct or actually rebuke the Prophet. Take this verse: "He frowned and turned away, because there came to him the blind man [interrupting]. But what could tell you but that perchance he might grow [in spiritual understanding]? Or that he might receive admonition, and the teaching might profit him? As to one who regards Himself as self-sufficient, to him do you attend; Though it is no blame to you if he grow not [in spiritual understanding]. But as to him who came to you striving earnestly, And with fear [in his heart], of him were you unmindful. By no means should it be so! For this is indeed a Message of instruction: Therefore let whoso will, keep it in remembrance" (80:1–12). The story behind this verse is that the Prophet was speaking to a Meccan chieftain about Islam, trying to win him over. A blind Muslim man, Ibn Um Maktum, interrupted the Prophet with a question. The Prophet became slightly annoyed with this, frowning and turning away from Ibn Um Maktum. God sent those verses to rebuke the Prophet and instruct the faithful. They have forevermore remained an example of the mindfulness and humility we should bring into all our relationships.

It is also interesting that the Prophet had no control over the timing of the revelation. For example, the Meccans had asked the Prophet some questions on the assumption that if he truly were a prophet of God, he would immediately know the answers. The Meccans learned of these questions from rabbis who lived in the city of Medina. The Prophet told them, "I will tell you tomorrow," expecting God to send the archangel Gabriel with the answers. The revelation did not come for fifteen days, during which time the skepticism of the Meccans grew and they began to speak ill about the Prophet, which saddened him deeply. When the revelation finally came with detailed answers to all their questions, the Qur'an rebuked the Prophet: "Do not ever say 'I shall be sure to do so and so tomorrow' without adding 'If God wills'; And call your Lord to mind when you forgettest, and say, 'I hope that my Lord will guide me ever closer [even] than this to the right road' " (18:23–24). If the Prophet was the author of the Qur'an, would he set himself up for ridicule on purpose? Furthermore, when the Hypocrites of Medina spread the rumor that the Prophet's wife Aisha had committed adultery, no revelation came for forty days. The rumors about his wife disturbed the Prophet deeply, and he himself wondered whether the allegations were true. The incident caused deep divisions among the Muslim community, and it would have been most convenient if a revelation were at hand. It took forty days before a revelation came that exonerated Aisha. This further debunks the notion that the author of the

Qur'an was Muhammad. The Qur'an, in fact, reiterates this
fact: "And you [O Muhammad] were not a reader of any scripture before, nor did you write it with your right hand, for then
might those who follow falsehood have doubted" (29:48).

During the time of the Prophet, as verses of the Qur'an were
revealed, they were memorized by the Prophet and a number
of his companions. These verses were spread orally, and several
Companions who could write did in fact write down the verses
for their own personal study. In addition, the Prophet would
dictate the verses revealed to him to scribes. The Prophet himself arranged the Qur'an in a specific order, and every year
during the month of Ramadan, he would review the entire revelation with the archangel Gabriel. In the year that the Prophet
died, he reviewed the revelations with Gabriel twice. After
the Prophet died, a number of Companions who memorized
the Qur'an were killed in the Battle of Yamama. One of the
Prophet's Companions, Umar ibn Al Khattab, told the Caliph
Abu Bakr that the Qur'an should be compiled into a single
book. Abu Bakr commissioned Zaid ibn Thabit to collect the
Qur'an into one book. Abu Bakr kept this copy with him, and
after he died, his successor, Umar, kept it, and after he took it,
Umar's daughter Hafsa kept it with her. At the time of the
Caliph Uthman, the Muslim nation was growing, and disputes
as to the correct recitation of the Qur'an had arisen. Thus, Uthman borrowed Hafsa's copy of the Qur'an and had scribes copy
it exactly. These copies were then distributed to the various
provinces of the Muslim lands, and all other copies in circula-
tion were destroyed. The authenticity of the text of Uthman
was agreed upon by consensus of all the Prophet's Companions.
This is the text used by Muslims today. The Qur'an is a very

sophisticated document, very forward thinking for seventh-century Arabia, as indicated by a verse like:

> He it is Who has sent down to you [O Muhammad] the Book: In it are verses basic or fundamental (of established meaning); they are the foundation of the Book: others are allegorical. But those in whose hearts is perversity follow the part thereof that is allegorical, seeking discord, and searching for its hidden meanings, but no one fully knows its hidden meanings except God. And those who are firmly grounded in knowledge say: 'We believe in the Book; the whole of it is from our Lord:' and none will grasp the Message except men of understanding. (3:7)

There are some verses that can be interpreted on many levels, and this has been an accepted part of Muslim tradition. It is essential, however, to know the fundamental verses: those that deal with God, the afterlife, and so forth. The Qur'an speaks about many things, but there are certain major themes that warrant discussion.

THE SIGNIFICANCE OF QUR'ANIC MONOTHEISM

First and foremost, the Qur'an is staunch in its monotheism, but what really is the significance of this? Was it really to contend with some mere primitive polytheism that this magnificent book was revealed? We miss the point if we think that the idolatry that is critiqued in the Qur'an has to do entirely with statues of wood and stone. The cumulative effect of the insights offered throughout the Qur'an is to awaken a sustained sense of the presence of God. The Qur'an establishes this awareness in the center of human consciousness where it belongs, not as a theological proposition requiring our conceptual assent, but as a living reality, a state of wonder, and an attitude of trust and surrender to the beneficence of God. "The false gods" are those self-created idols that displace this awareness of what is truly divine, in other words the idols of our own egoism, such as pride, ambition, control, greed, sensuality, and self-righteousness.

Throughout the Qur'an, the reality of God is stressed, insisted upon, and reiterated. Verses such as this abound: "Know, therefore, that there is no god but God, and ask forgiveness for your fault, and for the men and women who believe: for God knows how you move about and how you dwell in your homes" (47:19). This verse, called the Verse of the Throne, sums up the essence of who God is: "God! There is no god but He, the Living, the Self-subsisting, Eternal. Neither slumber nor sleep can seize Him. His are all things in the heavens and on earth. Who is there that can intercede in His presence except as He permits? He knows what [appears to His creatures as] before or after or behind them. Nor shall they compass aught of His knowledge except as He wills. His Throne extends over the heavens and the earth, and He feels no fatigue in guarding and preserving them for He is the Most High, the Supreme" (2:255). In addition, the Qur'an frequently discusses how and why there can only be one God:

> Say [O Muhammad]: Praise be to God, and Peace on his servants whom He has chosen [for his Message]. Who is better? God or the false gods they associate with Him? Or, Who has created the heavens and the earth, and

Who sends you down rain from the sky? Yes, with it We cause to grow well-planted orchards full of beauty of delight: it is not in your power to cause the growth of the trees in them. Can there be another god besides God? Nay, they are a people who swerve from justice. Or, Who has made the earth firm to live in; made rivers in its midst; set thereon mountains immovable; and made a separating isthmus between the two bodies of flowing water? Can there be another god besides God? No, most of them know not. Or, Who listens to the soul in distress when it calls on Him, and Who relieves its suffering, and makes you [mankind] inheritors of the earth? Can there be another god besides God? Little it is that you heed! Or, Who guides you through the depths of darkness on land and sea, and Who sends the winds as heralds of glad tidings, going before His Mercy? Can there be another god besides God? High is God above what they associate with Him! Or, Who originates creation, then repeats it, and who gives you sustenance from heaven and earth? Can there be another god besides Allah? Say, "Bring forth your argument, if you are telling the truth!" (27:59–64)

Notice that the Qur'an does not say, "I am One because I say so." The Qur'an goes to great lengths to address the intellect of the reader and cause him or her to reflect, frequently using examples from the natural world. In fact, the Qur'an has bemoaned the fact that people have not reflected upon and used their intellects with the Qur'an: "Do they not then earnestly seek to understand the Qur'an, or are their hearts locked up by them?" (47:24).

There have been those, as mentioned previously, who claim

that the God of Islam is not the Judeo-Christian God. They go as far as to say that the God of Islam is a distant, tribal, vicious, and violent God, devoid of love and mercy. In fact, it has been said—in so many words—that, in Islam, "God asks your son to die for Him," while in Christianity, "God sent His son to die for you." This is a very inaccurate notion of God in Islam. In Islam, Muslims have a direct, personal relationship with God Almighty. In the Qur'an, God says, "We have indeed created the human being and know what is whispered in his own self, and We are closer to him than his life pulse" (50:16). In another verse the Prophet Muhammad is told: "When My servants ask you concerning Me, I am indeed near: I answer the prayer of the one who prays to Me" (2:186). God in Islam is infinitely merciful. All but one of the 114 chapters of the Qur'an begin with the phrase: "In the Name of God, Most Gracious, Most Merciful." In one verse, God addresses humanity directly and says, "O my servants who have transgressed against themselves, despair not of the Mercy of God. For God forgives all sins, He is Oft-forgiving, Most Merciful" (39:53). Another example of God's mercy is how he doles out rewards for any good deeds: "He that doeth good shall have ten times as much to his credit: He that doeth evil shall only be recompensed according to his evil: no wrong shall be done unto [any of] them" (6:160).

The story of God's mercy is also outlined in detail in the sayings of the Prophet Muhammad. In one tradition, the Prophet said that if one were to come to God with the earth full of sins, God would come back with the earth full of forgiveness. In another saying, God forgave a prostitute simply because she gave a thirsty dog water to drink. The Prophet told us that all of the mercy we see on the earth, such as the love of a mother for her child, is a tiny fraction of the mercy God will show us on Judgment Day. In a particularly famous tradition, it is related that a man who murdered one hundred people was forgiven by God and admitted to paradise simply because he intended to change his evil ways. Islamic tradition is rich with descriptions of God's infinite mercy and forgiveness, and Muslims are comforted by the fact that any sin can be forgiven by God if the penitent is sincere in repentance.

LOVE OF GOD

In the Qur'an, God says: "Say [O Muhammad]: 'If you do love God, then follow me. God will love you and forgive your sins. For God is Oft-Forgiving, Most Merciful' " (3:31). In addition, numerous verses declare that God loves people for relying upon him, or for doing good, or for other reasons. Most importantly, God himself has declared that mercy is obligatory for him: "Say: 'To whom belongs all that is in the heavens and on earth?' Say: 'To God. He has inscribed for Himself [the rule of] Mercy. That He will gather you together for the Day of Judgment, there is no doubt whatever. It is they who have lost their own souls, that will not have faith' " (6:12).

If any Muslim teacher has given the impression that the God of Islam is not loving and merciful, it is a distortion of something absolutely fundamental to the faith. We must admit that the centrality of love has been neglected, overlooked, and even denied by some who claim to speak in the name of the religion. And yet the Qur'an itself gives this evidence that religion is essentially about love.

> O you who have attained to faith! If you ever abandon
> your faith, God will in time bring forth [in place of you]
> people whom He loves and who love Him—humble to-
> wards the believers, confident towards all who deny the
> truth: who strive hard in God's cause, and do not fear to
> be censured by anyone who might censure them: such is
> God's blessing, which He grants unto whom He wills.
> And God is infinite, all-knowing. (5:54)

What an extraordinary proclamation this is. We Muslims ourselves are warned that if we fail to keep the faith we have been given, we can be replaced. Not only that—we will be replaced by people *who love and who are loved by God.* This should be taken as clear scriptural evidence that love is of the essence.

In keeping with its staunch monotheism, the Qur'an rejects out of hand the notion that anything can share in the God-hood. Worshipping other gods besides God or joining partners with him is antithetical to everything for which Islam stands. In fact, the Qur'an is so stern against joining partners with God that several verses declare: "God forgives not that partners should be set up with Him; but He forgives anything else, to whom He pleases; to set up partners with God is to devise a sin most heinous indeed" (4:48). This being said, however, one who repents will find God most merciful. This stern stance against sharing the Godhood can also be found in the Bible: "For you shall worship no other god: for the Lord, whose name is Jealous, is a jealous God" (Exodus 34:14).

JESUS IN THE QUR'AN

Of course, the divinity of Jesus is firmly rejected: "O People of the Book [i.e., Christians]! Commit no excesses in your religion, nor say of God anything but the truth. Christ Jesus the son of Mary was a prophet of God, and His Word, which He bestowed on Mary, and a spirit proceeding from Him: so believe in God and His prophets. [But] say not 'Trinity': desist; it will be better for you: for God is one. Glory be to Him: far exalted is He above having a son. To Him belong all things in the heavens and on earth. And sufficient is God as a disposer of affairs" (4:171). Another verse says: "In blasphemy indeed are those that say that God is Christ the son of Mary. Say [O Muhammad]: 'Who then hath the least power against God, if His will were to destroy Christ the son of Mary, his mother, and everyone that is on the earth?' For to God belongs the dominion of the heavens and the earth, and all that is between. He creates what He pleases. For God hath power over all things" (5:17). Furthermore—and setting Islam apart from Christianity—the Qur'an denies that Jesus Christ died on the cross: "they killed him [Jesus] not, nor crucified him . . . surely they killed him not. But so it was made to appear to them" (4:157). Here is how the Qur'an expresses what happened to Jesus: "Behold! God said: 'O Jesus! I will take you and raise you to Myself and clear you [of the falsehoods] of those who blaspheme'" (3:55). In fact, the Qur'an says that God will ask Jesus if he ever called his people to worship him:

> And Lo! God said: "O Jesus, son of Mary! Did you say unto men, 'Worship me and my mother as deities beside God'?"
>
> He answered: "Limitless art You in Thy glory! It

would not have been possible for me to say what I had no right to say! Had I said this, You would indeed have known it! You know all that is within myself, whereas I know not what is in Your Self. Verily, it is You alone who fully knows all the things that are beyond the reach of a created being's perception. Nothing did I tell them beyond what You didst bid me [to say]: 'Worship God, [who is] my Sustainer as well as your Sustainer.' And I bore witness to what they did as long as I dwelt in their midst; but since You hast caused me to die, You alone hast been their keeper: for You are witness unto everything." (5:116–117)

Yet, despite firmly rejecting Jesus as divine, the Qur'an honors Jesus: "We gave him [Abraham] Isaac and Jacob: all [three] guided: and before him, We guided Noah, and among his progeny, David, Solomon, Job, Joseph, Moses, and Aaron: thus do We reward those who do good: And Zachariah and John, and Jesus and Elias: all in the ranks of the righteous" (6:84–85). Jesus Christ is considered one of the five mightiest prophets ever sent to humanity, along with Abraham, Noah, Moses, and Muhammad. The story of Jesus' virgin birth is recounted twice in the Qur'an. To Muslims, the miraculous virgin birth signals the greatness of Jesus as a prophet, not a sign of his divinity. In fact, Jesus is mentioned twenty-seven times in the Qur'an, more than six times as many as Muhammad himself. Jesus' miracles are detailed several times in the Qur'an. Here is one such passage:

Then will God say [on Judgment Day]: "O Jesus the son of Mary! Recount My favor to you and to your mother.

Behold! I strengthened you with the Holy Spirit, so that
you did speak to the people in childhood and in maturity.
Behold! I taught you the Book and Wisdom, the Law
and the Gospel and behold! You made out of clay, as it
were, the figure of a bird, by My leave, and you breathed
into it and it [became] a bird by My leave, and you healed
those born blind, and the lepers, by My leave. And behold! You brought forth the dead by My leave. And behold! I did restrain the Children of Israel from [violence
to] you when you didst show them the clear Signs, and
the unbelievers among them said: "This is nothing but
evident magic." (5:110)

In addition, the story of the Last Supper is also told in the
Qur'an (5:112–115).

THE VIRGIN MARY IN THE QUR'AN

Not only is Jesus Christ prominent in the Qur'an, the Virgin
Mary is also greatly revered. The story of her birth is recounted
in the Qur'an (3:35), and the Qur'an states: "Right graciously
did her Lord accept her: He made her grow in purity and
beauty" (3:37). In another verse, the Qur'an says, "Behold! The
angels said: 'O Mary! God hath chosen you and purified you
and chosen you above the women of all nations'" (3:42). In
fact, God portrayed the Virgin Mary as an example for the
ideal believer in the Qur'an: "And God sets forth, as an example to those who believe . . . Mary the daughter of 'Imran,
who guarded her chastity" (66:11–12). An entire chapter (chapter 19) is named after the Virgin Mary.

Muslims, like Christians, believe Jesus will return to earth again. This is not explicitly mentioned in the Qur'an, but it is hinted at in this verse: "And there is none of the People of the Book but must believe in him [Jesus] before his death; and on the Day of Judgment he will be a witness against them" (4:159). In another verse, the Qur'an says, "And [Jesus] shall be a Sign [for the coming of] the Hour [of Judgment]: therefore have no doubt about the [Hour], but follow Me: this is a Straight Way" (43:61). Muslim commentators have suggested that this verse refers to the return of Jesus Christ to the earth.

MOSES

Along with Jesus, the Qur'an speaks a great deal about Moses. In fact, about seventy-three passages—some encompassing several verses at a time—deal with Moses. Moses, just like Jesus, is also mentioned far more times in the Qur'an than Muhammad. The Qur'an says that God bestowed his grace upon Moses and Aaron (37:114), that he was "specially chosen" by God (19:51), and that God bestowed upon Moses "wisdom and knowledge" (28:14) as a reward for doing good. In addition, the Book of Moses is described by the Qur'an as a "Light and a Guidance" (6:91). One of the greatest blessings bestowed upon Moses was that God spoke to him directly: "and to Moses God spoke directly" (4:164). The Qur'an relates almost the entire story of Moses: from his birth to how he came to be reared in the house of Pharaoh, to how he killed an Egyptian, causing him to leave Egypt (28:3–46). The encounter between Moses and Pharaoh is retold in the Qur'an multiple times. Indeed, the Qur'an tells of two miracles—Moses' staff turning into a serpent and his hand glowing when he places it under his arm—that God permitted as proof of Moses' prophethood. It details the plagues that were unleashed on the Egyptians for their faithlessness and for enslaving the Hebrews (7:133), and the story of the golden calf is also mentioned (20:82–99). The splitting of the Red Sea is mentioned at least twice in the Qur'an (2:50, 26:52–68). In addition, the Qur'an details an encounter between Moses and a learned man who taught him about the knowledge and wisdom of God (18:60–82). To our knowledge, this story is not found in the Bible.

ABRAHAM

Abraham is also highly regarded in the Qur'an and is mentioned multiple times—again, several times more than Muhammad himself. There is an entire chapter of the Qur'an entitled "Ibrahim," Arabic for Abraham. The Qur'an has nothing but praise for the patriarch: "Surely Abraham was an exemplar, obedient to God, upright, and he was not an idolater. He was grateful for God's favors; God chose and guided him on the right path" (16:120–121). In another verse, God describes Abraham as a "close friend" (4:125). The Qur'an casts Abraham as a beautiful example of a believer: "Indeed, there is for you a beautiful example in Abraham and those with him" (60:4). He had unwavering faith in God, and he was ready to do whatever God commanded of him. The most prominent example of this was his willingness to sacrifice his only son—Ishmael in Islamic belief—in obedience to God (37:99–111). The Qur'an recounts the encounter between Abraham and King Nimrod, who challenged Abraham in matters of theology

(2:258), and it also tells the story of how Abraham's people attempted to burn him alive for preaching the worship of the One God: "They said, 'Burn him and protect your gods, If you do anything at all!' " (21:68) God, however, intervened and saved the patriarch: "O Fire! Be you cool, and a means of safety for Abraham!" (21:69).

Much of Islamic ritual traces its origin to Abraham. The Hajj was first started by Abraham, who had been told by God: "And proclaim among the people the pilgrimage: they will come to you on foot and every riding animal, coming from every remote path" (22:27). Islam's second major holiday, Eid Al Adha (Feast of the Sacrifice), commemorates Abraham's sacrifice of his son. On this holiday, Muslims sacrifice a lamb, just as Abraham sacrificed a ram in Ishmael's stead. The Qur'an maintains that Islam is essentially the same religion that Abraham followed: "Then we revealed to you [O Muhammad]: follow the religion of Abraham, the upright one" (16:123).

There are many other prophets mentioned in the Qur'an, twenty-five of them by name. Most are the Hebrew prophets, including Ishmael, Isaac, Jacob, Joseph, Elias, Elisha, Jethro, John the Baptist, and Jesus Christ. The entire story of Joseph, in fact, is recounted in the Chapter of Yusuf, and though it is essentially similar to the biblical account, it has even more detail of a spiritual nature.

In addition to these, the Qur'an tells the story of two ancient Arab prophets, Hud and Salih, not found in the Bible. As mentioned previously, all of the prophets of God are accorded reverence and respect. No devout Muslim would even fathom attacking the character or person of Jesus as some Christians have attacked the person of Muhammad.

ADAM AND EVE

The creation story is mentioned several times, and the Qur'an—in contrast to the biblical account—does not say that Eve "tempted" Adam to eat of the forbidden fruit. They both committed the sin together:

> We said: "O Adam! Dwell with your wife in the Garden; and eat of the bountiful things therein as you will; but approach not this tree, or run into harm and transgression." Then did Satan make *them* slip from the garden, and get them out of the state of felicity in which they had been. We said: "Get you down, all of you, with enmity between yourselves. On earth will be our dwelling-place and your means of livelihood for a time." (2:35–36) [emphasis added]

The stories of Noah's Ark and of David and Goliath are also related in the Qur'an, as are the fate of Sodom and Gomorrah, as well as the story of Jonah and the large fish.

Along with recounting the stories of the prophets of old, the Qur'an is also a legislative document, and it details laws concerning diet, ritual practice, inheritance, divorce, marital relations, criminal law, finance, and many other matters. For instance, the Qur'an prohibits the consumption of alcohol (as mentioned previously) and the flesh of swine: "O you who believe! Eat of the good things that We have provided for you, and be grateful to God, if it is Him you worship. He hath only forbidden you carrion, and blood, and the flesh of swine, and that on which any other name hath been invoked besides that of God. But if one is forced by necessity, without willful disobedience, nor transgressing due limits, then is he guiltless. For God is Oft-forgiving, Most Merciful" (2:172–173).

THE ORIGIN OF EVIL

The Qur'an teaches that Satan rebelled against God out of haughty arrogance. He was in heaven before Adam was created. He was, in fact, one of God's most pious servants. He even taught the angels. He was not an angel, but a member of the race of the *jinn,* an alternate creation of God. When Adam was created by God, God ordered everyone in heaven to bow down before Adam. All obeyed except Satan: "And behold, We said to the angels: 'Bow down to Adam' and they bowed down. Not so Iblis (Arabic for Satan): he refused and was haughty; He was of those who reject Faith" (2:34). Due to his rebellion against God, Satan was cast out of the Divine Presence in paradise. Satan, for his part, vowed to take humanity with him to hell:

> [God] said: "What prevented you from bowing down when I commanded you?" He said: "I am better than he: You did create me from fire, and him from clay." [God] said: "Get you down from this: it is not for you to be arrogant here: get out, for you are of the meanest [of creatures]." He said: "Give me respite till the day they are raised up." [God] said: "Be you among those who have respite." He said: "Because you have thrown me out of the way, lo! I will lie in wait for them on your straight way: Then will I assault them from before and behind, from their right and their left: Nor will you find, in most

of them, gratitude [for your mercies]." [God] said: "Get
out from this, disgraced and expelled. If any of them follow you, will I fill Hell with you all." (7:12–18)

The first person he "assaulted" on the path was none other than
Adam, as mentioned previously. In Islamic belief, angels cannot but obey God: it is not in their nature to disobey him.

Despite this vow by Satan to corrupt the human being, however, any evil that is committed by the human being is not because "the devil made him do it." This will not count with God
on Judgment Day. All Satan does is whisper and suggest; it is
the human being who makes the final decision, and as a result,
he or she must face the consequences. The Qur'an depicts a
scene before God on the day of judgment that illustrates this
point: "His Companion [the Devil] will say: 'Our Lord! I did
not make him transgress, but he was himself far astray.' God
will say: 'Dispute not with each other in My Presence: I had already in advance sent you warning' " (50:27–28). Furthermore,
when Satan and those who follow him are being punished in
hell, he will "indemnify" himself against all liability: "And Satan will say when the matter is decided: 'It was God Who gave
you a promise of Truth: I too promised, but I failed in my
promise to you. I had no authority over you except to call you,
but you listened to me: then reproach me not, but reproach
your own souls. I cannot listen to your cries, nor can you listen
to mine. I reject your former act in associating me with God.
For wrong-doers there must be a grievous penalty' " (14:22).
The Qur'an prescribes a remedy for protection from the whis-
pers of the devil: "If a suggestion from Satan assail your mind,
seek refuge with Allah, for He hears and knows [all things]"
(7:200). Furthermore, God declares that the machinations of

Satan are of no avail to the righteous servant: "For over My servants no authority shall you have, except such as put themselves in the wrong and follow you" (15:42).

The Qur'an repeatedly calls upon the human being not to follow in the "footsteps of Satan" (2:208, 2:168, 24:21). In fact, God reminds humanity of Adam's mistake, so that it might not be repeated: "O Children of Adam! Let not Satan seduce you, in the same manner as He got your parents out of the Garden, stripping them of their raiment, to expose their shame: for he and his tribe watch you from a position where you cannot see them: We made the Devils friends [only] to those without faith" (7:27). As a result, the Qur'an is full of exhortations to upright and moral conduct:

> It is not righteousness that you turn your faces towards East or West; but it is righteousness to believe in God and the Last Day, and the Angels, and the Book, and the Messengers; to spend of your substance, out of love for Him, for your kin, for orphans, for the needy, for the wayfarer, for those who ask, and for the ransom of slaves; to be steadfast in prayer, and practice regular charity; to fulfill the contracts which you have made; and to be firm and patient, in suffering and adversity, and throughout all periods of panic. Such are the people of truth and who are conscious of God. (2:177)

The proper attributes of the believer are expounded in moral terms: "The believers must [eventually] prevail: those who humble themselves in their prayers, and who avoid vain talk, and who are active in deeds of charity" (23:1–4). In one particularly moving passage, God describes "the servants of the Most Merciful" this way:

> And the servants of the Most Merciful are those who walk on the earth in humility, and when the ignorant address them, they say, "Peace!"; They are those who spend the night in adoration of their Lord, prostrate and standing; They are those who say, "Our Lord! avert from us the Wrath of Hell, for its Wrath is indeed an affliction grievous. Evil indeed is it as an abode and a place for rest." They are those who, when they spend, are not extravagant and not miserly, but hold a just balance between those extremes; They are those who do not invoke any other god with God, nor slay such life as God has made sacred except for just cause, nor commit fornication. (25:63–68)

In chapter 31, the Qur'an further lets the reader "eavesdrop" on a conversation between a wise man and his son, teaching him proper moral conduct in the process:

> Behold, Luqman said to his son by way of instruction: "O my son! Join not in worship others with God. For false worship is indeed the highest wrong-doing . . . O my son, if there were the weight of a mustard-seed and it were hidden in a rock, or anywhere in the heavens or on earth, God will bring it forth, for God understands the finest mysteries, and is well-acquainted with them. O my son, establish regular prayer, enjoin what is just, and forbid what is wrong: and bear with patient constancy what-

ever befalls you; for this is firmness in affairs. And swell not your cheek [for pride] at men, nor walk in insolence through the earth; for God does not love any arrogant boaster. And be moderate in your pace, and lower your voice; for the harshest of sounds without doubt is the braying of the ass." (31:13–19)

In the midst of the conversation between Luqman and his son, God interjects another extremely important injunction in the Qur'an: duty to one's parents: "And We have enjoined goodness to parents: in travail upon travail did his mother bear him, and in years twain was his weaning: [hear the command], 'Show gratitude to Me and to your parents: to Me is your final Goal' " (31:14). In this verse, as in others, the command to be grateful to one's parents comes immediately after gratitude to God. The juxtaposition in the Arabic text is not accidental: it is an indication of the importance of being kind to one's parents. Not only is one to be kind to parents, but the Qur'an goes further: "Your Lord hath decreed that you worship none but Him, and that you be kind to parents. Whether one or both of them attain old age in your life, say not to them a word of contempt, nor repel them, but address them in terms of honor. And, out of kindness, lower to them the wing of humility, and say: 'My Lord! bestow on them your Mercy even as they cherished me in childhood' " (17:23–24). The Muslim must be kind to his parents, even if they are not Muslim themselves. And even if one's parents actively strive against one's belief in God, the Qur'an is clear about this situation: "But if they strive to make you worship others besides Me, obey them not; *yet bear them company in this life with justice [and consideration],* and follow the way of those who turn to me [in love]: in the end the return of you all is to Me, and I will tell you the truth of all that you did" (31:15) [emphasis added]. Parents are not to be maltreated, no matter the circumstance.

JUSTICE

Another very important theme of the Qur'an is the importance of the establishment of justice on earth. Muslims are commanded by the Qur'an to stand up for justice: "Say: 'My Lord hath commanded justice'" (7:29). This stance must be unwavering, no matter what the circumstance: "O you who believe! Stand out firmly for justice, as witnesses to God, even against yourselves, or your parents, or your kin, and whether it be against rich or poor: for God can best protect both. Follow not the lusts [of your hearts], lest you swerve, and if you distort [justice] or decline to do justice, verily God is well-acquainted with all that you do" (4:135). Note that the Qur'an says that the Muslim must stand up for justice, even if it is against himself or his own parents. Furthermore, even the hatred of others toward you cannot lead you to commit injustice: "O you who believe, stand out firmly for God, as witnesses to fair dealing, and let not the hatred of others toward you make you swerve to wrong and depart from justice. Be just: that is next to piety: and fear God. For God is well-acquainted with all that you do" (5:8).

When the Muslims were in control of Mecca, God strictly forbade them from transgressing against the Meccans, even though they had bitterly persecuted the Muslims previously, because that would have been unjust:

O you who believe! Violate not the sanctity of the sym-
bols of God, nor of the sacred month, nor of the animals
brought for sacrifice, nor the garlands that mark out such
animals, nor the people resorting to the sacred house,
seeking the bounty and good pleasure of their Lord. But
when you are clear of the sacred precincts and of pilgrim
garb, you may hunt. Do let not the hatred of some people who once shut you out of the Sacred Mosque lead you
to transgression. Help one another in righteousness and
piety, but help not one another in sin and rancour: fear
God. For God is strict in punishment. (5:2)

This command to do justice extends to every facet of one's life:
justice in the marriage relationship; justice in business dealings:
"Give full measure when you measure, and weigh with a balance that is straight: that is the most fitting and the most ad-
vantageous in the final determination" (17:35).

The Qur'an tells a story of King David to remind the reader
of the importance of justice:

Has the Story of the Disputants reached you? Behold,
they climbed over the wall of the private chamber. When
they entered the presence of David, and he was terrified
of them, they said: "Fear not: we are two disputants, one
of whom has wronged the other: Decide now between us
with truth, and treat us not with injustice, but guide us to
the even Path. This man is my brother: He has nine and
ninety ewes, and I have but one: Yet he says, 'Commit her
to my care,' and is moreover harsh to me in speech."
David said: "He has undoubtedly wronged you in demanding your ewe to be added to his ewes: truly many are

the partners who wrong each other: Not so do those who believe and work deeds of righteousness, and how few are they?" . . . and David gathered that We had tried him: he asked forgiveness of his Lord, fell down, bowing, and repented. So We forgave him this lapse: he enjoyed, indeed, a Near Approach to Us, and a beautiful place of Final Return. (38:21–25)

What was the moral of this story? King David—and by extension all of us—must act with justice: "O David! We did indeed make you a viceregent on earth: so judge between men in truth: Nor follow the lusts [of your heart], for they will mislead you from the Path of God. For those who wander astray from the Path of God is a penalty severe, for that they forget the Day of Reckoning" (38:26). This stern command to do justice extends from the fact that God himself is just: "Every soul that hath sinned, if it possessed all that is on earth, would fain give it in ransom: They would declare their repentance when they see the penalty: but the judgment between them will be with justice, and no wrong will be done unto them" (10:54). Another passage states: "We shall set up scales of justice for the Day of Judgment, so that not a soul will be dealt with unjustly in the least, and if there be the weight of a mustard seed, We will bring it to account: and sufficient are We to take account" (21:47).

Since God is just, he expects no less from his servants, and this message is constantly repeated in the Qur'an.

The Qur'an is a book "without doubt," which contains "sure guidance for those who are conscious of God" (2:2). It is a book of laws; a book of moral injunctions; a book of spiritual comfort and strength; a book of sacred stories. It is the lasting miracle and legacy of the Prophet Muhammad. Yet, there is another legacy of the Prophet, his Sunnah, or the example of his behavior. Indeed, the Prophet told his followers, during his last sermon, that he had "left two things which, if you hold fast to them, you will never be misguided: the Book of God and my example." Yet with the death of the Prophet came the challenge of preserving his example for the generations of Muslims to come. This spurred an entire literature in Islamic scholarship: the hadith literature.

5

Hadith

In the Footsteps of the Prophet

The word "hadith" has a number of meanings in the Arabic language: "news," "tale," "story," or "report." Ask a Muslim what "hadith" means, and it is likely he or she will tell you that a hadith is a statement or saying of the Prophet. Typically, a hadith will read like this: "On the authority of . . . the Messenger of God (peace be upon him) said . . ." Sometimes, the chain of narrators is long; other times the chain is very short. An example of a hadith is this one, as reported in the collection of Imam Bukhari and Imam Muslim: "On the authority of Abu Hurayrah, the Messenger of God said, 'Let him who believes in God and the Last Day either speak good or keep silent, and let him who believes in God and the Last Day be generous to his neighbor, and let him who believes in God and the Last Day be generous to his guest.' " Abu Hurayrah was the Companion of the Prophet who heard the Prophet make the above statement. Imam Bukhari and Imam Muslim are the two most prominent collectors of sayings of the Prophet. It is generally accepted that the sayings of the Prophet contained in those collections are authentic. Yet the process that resulted in the collections of Bukhari and Muslim was several centuries in the making.

During the Prophet's lifetime, his Companions strove to memorize and remember everything he did and said. Since Muslims believe he was divinely guided and inspired, everything he did and said must be a source of guidance. Some of the Prophet's Companions had written down various sayings for their own study. These collections are called *Sahifas*. After the death of the Prophet, some of his Companions had scattered throughout the lands where Islam had spread. The Muslims in those lands were very eager to learn about the sayings and deeds of the Prophet. Out of these Muslims came the Successors, or the students of the Companions. It is these students who helped propagate the study of hadith among succeeding generations of Muslims. Large numbers of students attended the lectures on the sayings of the Prophet. Many of these were extremely pious and studious, and some of them became the sources of hadith literature.

Yet, sadly, an enormous number of hadith had been forged, likely beginning during the time of the Prophet himself. As time passed, the forging of Prophetic hadith became more and more commonplace. In fact, there is a whole subspecialty in hadith scholarship that deals with nothing but the forged sayings of the Prophet. Some people forged hadith for sectarian purposes, others for political expediency, still others to lend credibility to their heretical religious views. In fact, the most dangerous forgers were, ironically, the most pious Muslims. These Muslims forged various hadith to improve the piety of the general public. Yet this religious zeal proved to be very counterproductive because it made the task of differentiating authentic sayings of the Prophet from fabricated ones nearly impossible. Despite this widespread forgery of hadith, however, there remained a faithful core of honest scholars who dedicated their lives to the authentication of the sayings of the Prophet.

This faithful core of scholars took pains to point out the unreliability of anyone who forged hadith. They traveled far and wide throughout the Muslim world, even if it was in pursuit of a single saying of the Prophet. Eventually, this effort bore fruit, and various hadith collections began to emerge. The earliest of these were the *musnads*, which include that of Al Tayalisi, and Ahmad ibn Hanbal. The most important collections of hadith, as mentioned previously, were those of Bukhari and Muslim. Bukhari was a Persian scholar, and he dedicated more than one-quarter of his life to compiling his collection of hadith. Out of 600,000 hadith, he selected some 7,275 for his collection. The effort he exerted was nothing less than extraordinary, and Muslims continue to benefit from the fruits of his labor to this day. The collection of Bukhari is considered by most Muslims as second in authority only to the Qur'an itself. Almost simultaneously, the collection of Imam Muslim was being compiled. Muslim was a member of the Qushayr tribe of the Arabs. The collection of Imam Muslim is considered to be the most authentic collection of hadith after that of Imam Bukhari. Other important hadith collections include the Sunan of Abu Dawud, the Jami of al-Tirmidhi, and the Sunan of al-Nasa'i, al-Darimi, Ibn Maja, Daraqutni, Al Bayhaqi, and Ibn Mansur, among others. Although there are many collections, there are six hadith books that are considered the most sound.

In fact, they are called the "Sound Six": the collections of Bukhari, Muslim, Abu Dawud, al-Nasa'i, al-Tirmidhi, and Ibn Maja. The Shia have collections of hadith as well.

As a result of this extraordinary hadith scholarship, a number of subdisciplines emerged. Every hadith has a chain of narrators, or *isnad*. In order to deem a particular hadith authentic, the *isnad* must be confirmed, and this necessitates knowing the life, career, character, and scholarship of every member of the chain of narrators. This gave rise to the biographical dictionaries, which evaluated each hadith narrator. The earliest, and perhaps the most famous, of these dictionaries was the *Kitab al-Tabaqat al-Kabir* (Great Book of Classes) by Ibn Sa'ad. This dictionary was a general one, and more specific dictionaries were developed that studied the Prophet's Companions and hadith narrators from a specific city or town. Out of these dictionaries arose a discipline of hadith criticism. This criticism scrutinized both the reporters of hadith and the actual substance of the hadith themselves. Based on various criteria, hadith would then be considered *sahih*, or "sound," *hasan*, or "fair," or *da'if*, or "weak." There are a number of subcategories as well, and this meticulous cataloguing of hadith is essential to the science of Islamic jurisprudence, or Shariah.

The Qur'an says: "Believers, obey God, and obey the messenger; and don't let your actions be in vain" (47:33) and "So take whatever the messenger gives you, and refrain from anything he forbids you" (59:7). For the Muslims to obey the Messenger and take what he assigns them, they must know what he said. For them to know what he said, they must be reasonably sure that the words attributed to him were actually spoken by him. These needs gave birth to the entire hadith literature, and within two centuries, the major works of the literature had been compiled.

A COLLECTION OF SOUND HADITH

Islam

Every religion has a distinctive virtue, and the distinctive virtue of Islam is modesty.

Anyone who joins with a wrongdoer so that he may strengthen him, knowing all the while that he is a wrongdoer, has left Islam.

A Perfect Muslim

A perfect Muslim is someone from whose tongue and hands other people are safe, and a true emigrant [*mujahir*] is he who flees from what God has forbidden.

The messenger of God said to me [Anas], "Son, if you are able, from morning till night and from night till morning, keep your heart free from resentment toward anyone"; then he said, "Oh! My son, this is one of my laws, and he who loves my laws truly loves me."

The best of God's servants are those who, when seen, remind you of God; and the worst of God's servants are those who spread rumor, causing mischief and separating friends, and who search for the faults of the good.

He who believes in one God and the hereafter, let him speak what is good or remain silent.

That person is closest to God who forgives when he has someone in his power who would have injured him.

It is unworthy of a *mu'min* [a person of faith] to injure people's reputations; and it is unworthy to curse anyone, to abuse anyone, or to talk arrogantly.

All Muslims are like a single person. If one feels a pain in his head, his whole body feels pain; and if his eye is hurt, his whole body hurts.

All Muslims are like one foundation, some parts strengthening others; in such a way they support each other.

Assist your brother Muslim, whether he is an oppressor or one of the oppressed. "But what shall we do when he is an oppressor?" Muhammad said, "To assist an oppressor is to forbid and stop him from oppressing others."

The performance of religious duties will not atone for the fault of an abusive tongue. A man cannot be a Muslim till his heart and tongue are in submission.

Certainly, people will follow you, and come to you from all quarters of the earth to understand religion; when they come to you, guide them toward goodness.

The best *jihad* [literally, striving] is to speak a word of justice before a tyrant.

Your smiling in your brother's face is a gift of charity; and your encouraging people to virtuous deeds is charity; and your prohibiting the forbidden is charity; and your showing people the road when they have lost it is charity; and your assisting the blind is charity.

I came to Medina and saw a man whose counsels men obeyed, and whenever he said anything, they obeyed him. I said, "Who is this man?" They said, "This is the Prophet of God." Then I went to him and said, "Give me advice." The Prophet Muhammad said, "Abuse nobody." And I never abused anyone after that, neither freeman nor slave, nor camel nor goat. And he added, "And if a man abuse you, and reveal a vice which he knew in you, even then do not reveal one which you know in him."

God

God's kindness toward His creatures is more than a mother's toward her babe.

Truly, God is gentle, and he loves gentleness, and He gives to the gentle what he does not give to the harsh.

Truly God instructs me to be humble and modest and not vain, and let no one oppress others.

He who humbles himself for the sake of God, God will exalt; though he is small in his own mind, he is great in the eyes of the people. And whoever is arrogant and proud, God will bring him to contempt. He is small in the eyes of the people and great in his own mind, so that he becomes more contemptible to them than a dog or a pig.

God is a unity, and likes unity.

We were with the Prophet on a journey, and some men stood up repeating aloud, "God is most great"; and the Prophet said, "O men, be easy on yourselves and do not distress yourselves by raising your voices; truly, you do not call to one who is deaf or absent, but Truly to one who hears and sees; and he is with you; and He to whom you pray is nearer to you than the neck of your camel."

The most beloved of men in the sight of God, on the day of resurrection, and the nearest to Him, in regard to position, shall be the just leader; and the most hateful of men in the sight of God on the day of Resurrection, and the farthest removed from Him, shall be the tyrannical leader.

Faith

You will not enter paradise until you have faith; and you will not complete your faith till you love one another.

A man asked, "O Prophet of God! what is faith?" The Prophet said, "When your good work gives you pleasure, and your evil work grieves you, and you are a man of faith." The man said, "And what is sin?" he said, "Whatever disturbs your heart—forsake it."

Faith is a restraint against all violence, let no person of faith commit violence.

Any one of you who sees wrong, let him undo it with his hand; and if he cannot, then let him speak against it with his tongue; and if he cannot do this either, then let him abhor it with his heart, and this is the least of faith.

If you rely upon God as He ought to be relied upon, He will provide you as He provides the birds; they go out empty and hungry in the morning and come back with full stomachs in the evening.

Service to Humanity

He is true who protects his brother both present and absent.

What actions are most excellent? To gladden the heart of a human being, to feed the hungry, to help the afflicted, to lighten the sorrow of the sorrowful, and to remove the wrongs of the injured.

He who tries to remove the want of his brother, whether he be successful or not, God will forgive his sins.

The best of people is one from whom humanity benefits.

All God's creatures are His family; and he or she is the most beloved of God who tries to do most good to God's creatures.

Someone said to the Prophet, "Pray to God against the idolators and curse them." The Prophet replied, "I have been sent as a mercy; I have not been sent to curse."

Truly my heart is veiled with melancholy and sadness for my followers and verily I ask pardon of God one hundred times daily.

Words to Remember

The proud will not enter paradise, nor will a violent speaker.

God is not merciful to him who is not so to mankind.

Kindness is a sign of faith, and whoever has not kindness has not faith.

Anyone who kills a sparrow for nothing, it will cry aloud to God on the day of resurrection, saying, "O My Lord! such and such a man killed me for nothing, not for any good."

An adulteress who passed by a dog at a well holding out his tongue dying from thirst was forgiven; for she took off her short boot and tied it to her wrapper, and fetched water for him. She was pardoned for that. It was asked, "Shall we then have any reward for [our behavior to] the animals?" "There are rewards," said the Prophet, "for all those endowed with fresh and tender hearts."

We were on a journey with the Prophet when we saw a finch with two young ones. We took away the two young ones and the mother bird fluttered around. Then the Prophet came and said, "Who has distressed her by taking away her young ones? Return her young ones to her." The Prophet also saw the abode of ants which we had burnt,

and said, "Who has burnt this?" We said, "We have done
this." The Prophet said, "It is not proper that anyone
should punish another by fire unless it be the Lord of fire
himself."

General Advice

I found this inscribed on the hilt of the Prophet's sword:
"Forgive him who wrongs you; join him who cuts you off;
do good to him who does evil to you; and speak the truth
although it be against yourself."

The best of your leaders are those whom you love and who
love you, for whom you pray, and who pray for you; and
the worst of your leaders are those whom you hate, and
who hate you, whom you curse, and who curse you.

Muhammad said, "My Cherisher has ordered me nine
things: 1) to reverence Him, externally and internally; 2) to
speak true, and with propriety, in prosperity and adversity;
3) to be moderate in affluence and poverty; 4) to benefit my
relations and kindred who do not benefit me; 5) to give alms
to him who refuses me; 6) to forgive him who injures me;
7) that my silence should be in attaining knowledge of God;
8) that when I speak, I should mention Him; 9) that when I
look on God's creatures, it should be as an example for them."

Deal gently with the people, and be not harsh; cheer them
and do not condemn them.

Do not exceed bounds in praising me; I am only the Lord's
servant; then call me the servant of God and His messenger.

6

The Sum of All Fears

Freedom, Jihad, and Gender

The attacks of September 11, 2001, opened the floodgates of comment by pundits, commentators, and "experts" on the "true" nature of Islam, its holy scripture, and its Prophet. Islam has been called an "evil, wicked religion"; the Prophet has been called a "terrorist" and "a demon-possessed pedophile"; the Qur'an has been labeled a book of violence. This charge is perhaps the most oft repeated. Time and again, people claim the Qur'an orders Muslims to kill all non-Muslims. The fears of non-Muslims need to be addressed, both because adherents of some forms of ideological Islam are aggressively committing acts of arbitrary violence, but also because the media, certain people with political and/or religious axes to grind, and others who are just ignorant promote overly simplistic and negative stereotypes of Islam and Muslims.

On the other hand, some Muslims, especially those who have never been to a Western country, may have extreme views of what life is like in Europe or America. Unfortunately, there is an almost universal human tendency to project on the Other the "shadow" of our own culture, the unrecognized dark side of ourselves.

THE SANCTITY OF LIFE

First of all, the Qur'an is adamant that all human life is sacred: "Come, and I will declare what your Lord has forbidden you. You should not associate anything with God, you should be good to your parents, and not kill your children on account of poverty—We provide for you and for them. And do not approach indecencies, whether outward or inward. And do not kill a person—which God has made sacred—except in justice. Thus has God commanded you, that you may understand" (6:151). In another verse, God reiterates the stern prohibition against killing children for fear of want, further emphasizing the sanctity of human life in Islam: "Do not kill your children out of fear of poverty; We will provide for them and for you. Indeed, killing them is a great sin" (17:31). Elsewhere he warns: "And do not take a life that God has made sacred, except for just cause" (17:33). These verses are absolutely clear: no life can be taken without just cause, religious beliefs notwithstanding.

Moreover, in Islam suicide has been viewed as a denial of God's mercy, and it is unequivocally prohibited: "And do not kill yourselves; for God has been merciful to you" (4:29). There are a great number of traditions of the Prophet, contained in the most authentic of collections, that unabashedly condemn suicide. In fact, the Prophet said that the one who commits suicide will be condemned to continually repeating the act of suicide in the fires of hell. This stern stance against suicide is further evidence of the absolute sanctity of human life in Islam. Furthermore, the Qur'an has equated the taking of innocent life with taking the lives of all humanity, and it presents this as a fundamental moral principle that has been common to the Abrahamic faiths: "Because of that We ordained for the Children of Israel that if anyone killed a person, other than for murder or corruption on earth, it would be as if he killed all humanity" (5:32).

A RELIGION OF THE SWORD?

Now, there are a number of verses in the Qur'an that do call for Muslims to kill non-Muslims. Among these—and perhaps the most often cited—is the infamous "Verse of the Sword": "Kill idolaters [*mushrikeen*—those Meccans who had declared war against Muhammad and his community] wherever you find them, and capture them, and blockade them, and watch for them at every lookout" (9:5). On the surface, this verse would seem to bolster the claim that Islam advocates violence against non-Muslims. There is much more to this story, however. This verse, and the others like it in the Qur'an, have a linguistic, historical, and textual context. Understanding that context is essential in understanding the message of the verse. Careful and unbiased study of these verses, in their proper context, will reveal that the exhortations to fight "idolators" and "unbelievers" are specific in nature and are not general injunctions for the murder of all those who refuse to accept Islam as their way of life. We must remember the challenging historical circumstances of these Qur'anic verses.

As we discussed in the chapter outlining the Prophet's biography, the Meccan oligarchy fought against the Prophet's message from the very beginning. Its members resorted to violent repression and torture of the Prophet and his followers when they realized that the flow of converts to Islam was increasing. The Prophet himself survived several assassination attempts, and conditions became so dangerous for the Muslims in Mecca that the Prophet sent some of his Companions to take asylum in the Christian kingdom of Abyssinia. After thirteen years of violence, Muhammad was compelled to take refuge in the city of Medina, and even then the Meccans did not relent in their hostilities. Later, furthermore, various hostile Arab tribes joined in the fight against the Muslims, culminating in the Battle of the Trench, when ten thousand soldiers from many Arab tribes gathered to wipe out the Muslim community once and for all. As we know, the Muslims survived these challenges and eventually went on to establish a vast civilization.

At the time verse 9:5 of the Qur'an was revealed, Mecca had been conquered, the Meccans themselves had become Muslims, and many of the surrounding pagan Arab tribes had also accepted Islam and sent delegations to the Prophet pledging their allegiance to him. Those that did not become Muslim were the bitterest of enemies, and it was against these remaining hostile forces that the verse commands the Prophet to fight. It was in this violent context that the Verse of the Sword was revealed. This verse is part of a long chapter entitled "Repentance," and it was revealed nine years after the Prophet immigrated to Medina.

Yet, verse 9:5 must never be quoted out of context. The verses immediately before and after it explain why verse 9:5 ex-

horts the believers to "kill idolaters wherever you find them."
The first verses state: "There is immunity from God and the
messenger of God for those polytheists [*mushrikeen*] with
whom you have made treaties; So travel the earth for four
months, and know that you cannot elude God, and that it is
God who brings disgrace upon all who refuse to acknowledge
the truth" (9:1–2). The polytheists in these verses are those pagan Arabs who have deliberately broken the treaties they
forged with the Prophet. How do we know this? Verse 4 continues: "Except those polytheists with whom you have made a
treaty and who have not failed you in anything and have not
helped anyone against you; fulfill your treaties with them to the
end of their term, for God loves the conscientious." Had we
quoted only 9:1–2, without the qualifying verse 9:4, it would
seem that the Qur'an invalidates all nonaggression treaties
made with the non-Muslims so that they can be "slaughtered"
according to 9:5. That is clearly not the case. Those who want
to malign Islam quote only 9:1–2 and neglect to mention 9:4.

Now, in its proper context, verse 9:5 can be properly understood. In addition, most who quote 9:5 do so incompletely. The
full verse reads: "But when the sacred months are past, then kill
idolaters wherever you find them, and capture them, and
blockade them, and watch for them at every lookout. But if
they repent and practice prayer and give alms, then let them go
their way; for God is most forgiving, most merciful." This was
a specific command to the Prophet at that specific time to fight
those idolaters who were fighting the Muslims—those idolaters who, as 9:4 mentioned, failed in their treaty obligations
and helped others fight against the Muslims. It is not a general
command to attack all non-Muslims, and it has never signified

this to the overwhelming majority of Muslims throughout history. Had it been so, then every year, after the "forbidden months are past," history would have witnessed Muslims attacking every non-Muslim in sight. (The "forbidden months" are four months out of the year during which fighting is not allowed. Three of them occur in a row: the eleventh, twelfth, and first month of the Islamic calendar.) This yearly slaughter never occurred. In addition, if one reads on in the ninth chapter, the Qur'an further explains why 9:5 commands the Prophet to "kill idolaters wherever you find them": "If they get the better of you, they do not respect either blood relations or treaty with you. They satisfy you with their words, but their hearts are averse, and most of them are dissolute" (9:8). Further along the Qur'an declares: "Will you not fight people who broke their oaths and planned to exile the messenger, and they took the initiative the first time? Do you fear them? God is more worthy of your fear, if you are believers" (9:13). These pagan tribes, as the Qur'an clearly states, would not hesitate in the least to attack and kill the Muslims at their first chance, and thus they must be fought against. Furthermore, if 9:5 were a general exhortation to kill all non-Muslims, then verse 9:6 would make no sense: "And if one of the polytheists asks you for protection, then protect him, until he hears the word of God: then deliver him to a place safe for him. That is because they are people who do not know." Yet verse 9:6 does make sense because the command to "kill idolaters wherever you find them" refers solely to those who are in active hostility to the Muslims. Had verse 9:5 been an open invitation to kill all non-Muslims, it would have been more convenient for the verse to be revealed as soon as the Prophet arrived as leader in Medina, with an army of believers ready to fight to the death for him. Yet, as previously mentioned, the verse was revealed nine years after the Prophet came to Medina.

Another set of verses seemingly declares that all nonbelievers are to be attacked and killed:

> And let them not think—those who are bent on denying the truth [i.e., nonbelievers]—that they shall escape [God]: behold, they can never frustrate [His purpose]. Hence, make ready against them whatever force and war mounts you are able to muster, so that you might deter thereby the enemies of God, who are your enemies as well, and others besides them of whom you may be unaware, but of whom God is aware; and whatever you may expend in God's cause shall be repaid to you in full, and you shall not be wronged. (8:59–60)

Once again, the textual context must be examined. These two verses refer to those who are in active hostility against the Muslim community. An examination of the verses that come before these elucidates this point:

> As for those with whom you have made a covenant, and who thereupon break their covenant on every occasion, not being conscious of God—if you find them at war [with you], make of them a fearsome example for those who follow them, so that they might take it to heart; or, if you have reason to fear treachery from people [with whom you hast made a covenant], cast it back at them in an equitable manner: for, verily, God does not love the treacherous! (8:56–59)

When read together, it is clear that verses 8:59–60 speak of those nonbelievers who actively fight against the Muslims and break their covenants "every time." Again, there is no general exhortation to fight and kill all non-Muslims.

In yet another set of verses, the Qur'an tells the believers not once but twice to kill nonbelievers: "seize them and slay them wherever you may find them" (4:89) and "seize them and slay them whenever you come upon them: for it is against these that We have clearly empowered you [to make war]" (4:91). We deliberately quoted these two verses out of context to illustrate how deceitful and misleading such a practice is. Again, once the verses are understood in context, it is quite clear that these verses tell the Muslims to fight only those who fight them. First of all, these verses are part of a slightly longer passage that begins: "How, then, could you be of two minds about the hypocrites, seeing that God has disowned them because of their guilt? Do you, perchance, seek to guide those whom God has let go astray—when for him whom God lets go astray you can never find any way?" (4:88) The verse speaks of the "hypocrites," which raises the question of who these "hypocrites" are. They are those Muslims who feigned outward acceptance of Islam but secretly worked for the destruction of the Muslims. They constantly acted as a fifth column within the Muslim community in Medina. Chief among them, as we discussed earlier, was Abdullah ibn Ubay. This man worked continually to harm the Muslims. For example, on the way to the mountain of Uhud, where the second battle against the pagans in Mecca took place, Abdullah ibn Ubay told his followers to go back home because he did not think a battle was going to be waged. His followers, and some true, believing Muslims, obeyed him, and the Muslim army was cut by two-thirds, from a thousand men to approximately three hundred. During this battle, the Prophet was severely wounded and nearly killed by the Meccans.

Yet, despite the treachery of these nonbelievers verses 4:89 and 4:91 do not call on the Prophet to "kill them all," but only those who are in open hostility to him: "They [the hypocrites] would love to see you deny the truth even as they have denied it, so that you should be like them. Do not, therefore, take them for your allies until they forsake the domain of evil for the sake of God; and *if they revert to open enmity,* seize them and slay them wherever you may find them. And do not take any of them for your ally or giver of succor" (4:89) [emphasis added]. Furthermore, 4:90 explains that if these hypocrites do not fight the Muslims, they are not to be harmed: "Unless it be those that have ties with people to whom you yourselves are bound by a covenant, or such as come to you because their hearts shrink from [the thought of] making war either on you or on their own folk . . . thus, if they let you be, and do not make war on you, and offer you peace, God does not allow you to harm them." The same is true for the following verse, 4:91: "You will find others who would like to be safe from you as well as from their own folk, but who, whenever they are faced anew with temptation to evil, plunge into it headlong. Hence, *if they do not let you be, and do not offer you peace, and do not stay their hands,* seize them and slay them whenever you come upon them: for it is against these that We have clearly empowered you" [emphasis added]. Yet again, the Qur'an says to fight only those who fight against the Muslims.

It should be quite obvious by now that there is a recurring theme in the above verses: fighting is only in self-defense, and it is only against those who fight against the Muslims. Indeed,

Islam is a religion that seeks to maximize peace and reconciliation. Yet, Islam is not a pacifist religion; it does accept the premise that, from time to time and as a last resort, arms must be taken up in a just war. If Muslims are fought against, Islam demands that they fight back. Hence, one will find very belligerent verses in the Qur'an, such as the ones we quoted above. But, as we mentioned, these verses exist in a context and are specific in their scope. They are not general exhortations to violence. The Qur'an is quite clear about this. The verses concerning fighting that were revealed soon after the Prophet arrived in Medina are self-defensive in nature: "Victims of aggression are given license [to fight] because they have been done injustice; and God is well able to help them" (22:39). Why was this permission granted? The Qur'an continues: "[They are] those evicted from their homes without reason except that they say, 'Our Sustainer is God'" (22:40). Furthermore, when Muslims do fight in war, it's not with the attitude that "all is fair," as has been claimed. Islamic Law has always recognized principles of just war. Muslims are strictly forbidden to commit aggression: "And fight for the sake of God those who fight you; but do not be brutal or commit aggression, for God does not love brutal aggression" (2:190). The next verse also says, "slay them wherever you may come upon them," but if the entire verse is read, it is clear that the "slaying" is also in self-defense: "And slay them wherever you may come upon them, and drive them away from wherever they drove you away—for oppression is even worse than killing. And fight not against them near the Inviolable House of Worship [the Ka'ba] unless they fight against you there first; but if they fight against you, slay them: such shall be the recompense of those who deny the truth" (2:191). If the enemy inclines toward peace, however,

Muslims must follow suit: "But if they stop, God is most forgiving, most merciful" (2:192); "Now if they incline toward peace, then incline to it, and place your trust in God, for God is the all-hearing, the all-knowing" (8:61). Moreover, God insists that the Muslims should incline toward peace if their enemies do the same, even though the possibility might exist that the enemy is deceiving them: "And if they mean to deceive you, surely you can count on God, the one who strengthened you with Divine aid and with the believers" (8:62).

Even if those who fight against the believers are other believers, the Qur'an says that they should be fought against: "If two parties of believers contend with each other, make peace between them. Then if one of the two acts unjustly to the other, *fight the side that transgresses* until it goes back to the order of God" (49:9) [emphasis added]. Again, fighting is allowed only against those who transgress, those who fight against the believers. Indeed, the Qur'an explains why fighting and warfare are even allowed in God's plan. An important reason is to prevent oppression on the earth, in keeping with the Qur'an's strong insistence that justice be upheld: "Why would you not fight in the cause of God, and oppressed men, women, and children, who say, 'Our Lord, get us out of this town, whose people are oppressors. And provide us a protector from You, and provide us a helper from You'" (4:75). Yet, an equally important reason—and one that may come as a surprise to the reader—is to protect the free and unfettered worship of God:

> For if God did not parry people by means of one another,
> then monasteries and churches and synagogues and
> mosques—wherein the name of God is much recited—
> would surely be demolished. And God will surely defend

those who defend God—for God is powerful, almighty.
(22:40)

This is truly remarkable. The Qur'an endorses armed conflict, as a last resort, in order to protect Christian, Jewish, and Muslim houses of worship. So much for Islam's intolerance. This principle is further outlined in the following verse: "Hence, fight against them until there is no more oppression [*fitnah*, in Arabic] and all worship is devoted to God alone; but if they desist, then all hostility shall cease, save against those who [willfully] do wrong" (2:193). The verse states that Muslims should fight on until there is no more *fitnah*. And verse 2:191, cited above, says that "oppression [*fitnah*] is even worse than killing." What is this *fitnah*?

The word *fitnah* appears at least twenty-eight times in the Qur'an, and its use and meaning vary depending on the verse in question. Some classical commentators, particularly Ibn Kathir, have written that *fitnah*, especially in verse 2:193, denotes idolatry. As a result, those who wish to smear Islam allow the opinion of Ibn Kathir to speak for the text and claim that the Qur'an says: "Become Muslim or die." Yet the text of the Qur'an itself, and its use of the word *fitnah*, do not agree with this scholar's interpretation. For example, in quite a few verses, *fitnah* means "trial" or "tribulation": "And know that your possessions and your children are but a trial [*fitnah*], and that there is a higher reward in the presence of God" (8:28) and "Every living being tastes death: and We try you with ill and good as a test [*fitnah*]; and you will be returned to Us" (21:35). Yet another verse says: "All the emissaries We sent before you did eat food and walked along the streets. And We made some of you a trial [*fitnah*] for others; will you be forbearing? For your Lord is all-seeing" (25:20). In other verses, *fitnah* means corruption and discord (9:47–48). Now, in verse 33:14, *fitnah* does indeed mean apostasy: "But if they were invaded from the sides, then asked to dissent and join in civil war ["asked for *fitnah*," in Arabic], they would do so with but little delay" (33:14). The "they" in this verse refers to the Hypocrites, whom we discussed earlier. The use of the word *fitnah* here, however, cannot be generalized to every other verse in the Qur'an. Verse 2:193, which exhorts the believers to "fight against them until there is no more *fitnah*, and all worship is devoted to God alone" must be understood in context. This verse comes after verse 2:190, which commands the believers to fight those who fight them, i.e., the hostile Arabs who stopped at nothing to be the first to draw Muslim blood. In addition, these people, especially the Meccan oligarchy, violently persecuted any new converts to Islam and prevented the free worship of God by these Muslims. It is to this religious persecution, we believe, that the word *fitnah* in 2:193 refers. This definition of *fitnah* is supported by another verse, which responded to the Meccans' claim that the Prophet does not honor the sanctity of the sacred months. Recall that the Muslims mistakenly killed a Meccan during one of the sacred months, when fighting between enemies is strictly forbidden. The verse reads: "They ask you [O Muhammad] about fighting in the sacred month. Say, 'Fighting then is an offense; but more offensive to God is blocking the way to the path of God, denying God, preventing access to the sacred mosque, and driving out its people. And persecution [*fitnah*] is worse than killing' " (2:217). Again, here the *fitnah* about which the verse is speaking means preventing access to the path of God and his sacred mosque, driving out the believers from Mecca, and even denying God himself. All this is the violent repression of religious freedom, and this must be prevented, even if it means armed conflict. Again, this whole discussion about fighting until there is no more *fitnah* follows the same theme of fighting only in self-defense. A more careful analysis of the Qur'an—in its proper historical, linguistic, and textual context—clearly shows that it does not give a general, time-honored exhortation to kill all non-Muslims. That Islam calls for a "war on unbelievers" is sheer fallacy and utter fantasy.

RELATIONS WITH OTHER FAITHS

There are also charges that the Qur'an is derogatory toward Christians and Jews, called "People of the Book," or "people of scripture." Some have claimed that the Qur'an says Jews are consigned to "ignominy and humiliation" (2:61), are "cursed" and try to introduce corruption (5:64), have always been disobedient (5:78), and are enemies of God (2:97–98). Most distressingly, Islam's detractors claim that the Qur'an calls for the murder of Christians and Jews, and they cite this verse: "Fight the ones among those to whom scripture has been given who do not have faith in God and the last day, and do not consider inviolable what God and God's messenger have made inviolable, and do not profess the religion of truth, until they pay tribute willingly, as subjects" (9:29). Again, when one is studying verses that, on the surface, seem to be utterly derogatory and even violent toward Jews and Christians, the historical and textual context must be examined carefully.

First, let us take up verse 2:61. The verse does talk about the children of Israel and contains the words "ignominy and humiliation." Yet these two words are a tiny portion of the verse.

In the verse, God is addressing the children of Israel directly, reminding them of their sacred history: "And [remember] when you said, 'O Moses, indeed we cannot endure but one kind of food; pray then, to thy Sustainer that He bring forth for us something of what grows from the earth—of its herbs, its cucumbers, its garlic, its lentils, its onions.' And Moses said: 'Would you take a lesser thing in exchange for what is so much better? Go back in shame to Egypt, and then you can have what you are asking for!' And so, ignominy and humiliation overshadowed them, and they earned the burden of God's condemnation: all this, because they persisted in denying the truth of God's messages and in slaying the prophets against all right: all this, because they rebelled [against God] and persisted in transgressing the bounds of what is right." Does this verse speak about all Jews? Absolutely not. It speaks of those Jews who were contentious with Moses, a prophet of God.

Verse 5:64 says:

> And the Jews say the hand of God is bound. But it is *their* hands that are bound, and they are accursed, by what they say. No, the hands of God are free, openly giving at will. But what has been revealed to you from your Lord will increase them in their overweening arrogance and in their denial of the truth. And so We have cast enmity and hatred between them until the day of resurrection. Every time they kindle the fire of war, God extinguishes it; yet they strive to spread corruption on earth: and God does not love the spreaders of corruption.

This verse speaks of those Jews in Medina who uttered a word of blasphemy against God, namely that God's Hands are "bound" or stingy with His bounty upon the Muslims. They said this to assert that the Muslims must not be the true followers of God, since they were in abject poverty in Medina and God should have bestowed upon the Muslims an abundance of riches. God, in this verse, sought to correct this faulty claim in, admittedly, very harsh terms. Yet, this is not a smear against all Jews. This verse is a specific response to a specific charge by the Jews of Medina.

The verse does go on to say "we have cast enmity into their hearts until the Day of Resurrection," and this is addressed to both Christians and Jews, but not necessarily to all Jews or Christians. It addresses rather only those who have fallen away from the truth given to them in their own scriptures. For the following verses say:

> If the followers of the Bible would but attain to [true] faith and God-consciousness, We should indeed efface their [previous] bad deeds, and indeed bring them into gardens of bliss; and if they would but truly observe the Torah and the Gospel and all [the revelation] that has been bestowed from on high upon them by their Sustainer, they would indeed partake of all the blessings of heaven and earth. Some of them do pursue a right course; but as for most of them—vile indeed is what they do! (5:65–66)

Later on in the fifth chapter, we read these verses: "Those of the Children of Israel who were bent on denying the truth were cursed by the tongue of David and Jesus, Son of Mary; that was because they were defiant and they used to commit outrages. They never used to forbid one another from the abominations they committed. Evil indeed is what they used to do" (5:78–79). Are these verses saying that all Jews are cursed and disobedient? Again, absolutely not. Read the verses more carefully: they say that it was King David and Jesus Christ who had cursed *those who denied the truth* from among the children of Israel. It was this rebellious subset that was disobedient and failed to prevent the commission of iniquity. There is evidence of this fact in the Bible. In the Psalms, we read verses 78:18–22, which say:

> And they tempted God in their heart by asking meat for their lust. Yea, they spoke against God; they said, Can God furnish a table in the wilderness? Behold, he smote the rock, and the waters gushed out, and the streams overflowed; can he give bread also? Can he provide flesh for his people? Therefore the Lord heard this, and was angry: so a fire was kindled against Jacob, and anger also came up against Israel; Because they believed not in God, and trusted not in his salvation.

In the New Testament, Jesus is approached by disciples of the Pharisees, and they ask him, "Tell us therefore, What do you think? Is it lawful to give tribute unto Caesar, or not? *But Jesus perceived their wickedness, and said, Why do you tempt me, you hypocrites?*" (Matthew 22:17–18) [emphasis added]. In Matthew 23, Jesus repeatedly calls the scribes and Pharisees "hypocrites," and he goes even further than that: "You serpents, you generation of vipers, how can you escape the damnation of hell?" (Matthew 23:33). Also, Jesus says in Matthew 12:34: "O generation of vipers, how can you, being evil, speak good things? For out of the abundance of the heart the mouth speaks." Furthermore, Jesus talks about Jerusalem and the slaying of the prophets just as the Qur'an does: "O Jerusalem, Jerusalem, you that kills the prophets, and stones them which are sent unto you, how often would I have gathered thy children together, even as a hen gathers her chickens under her wings, and you would not!" (Matthew 23:37).

Verses 2:97–98 do not disparage the Jews either. They read as follows:

> Say [O Muhammad]: "Whosoever is an enemy of Gabriel—who, verily, by God's leave, has brought down upon your heart this [divine writ] which confirms the truth of whatever there still remains [of earlier revelations], and is a guidance and glad tiding for the believers—whosoever is an enemy of God and His angels and His messengers, and Gabriel [or] Michael, should know that, verily, God is the enemy of all who deny the truth."

The story behind the revelation of these verses is that a company of Jews had asked the Prophet which angel sent down the revelations from God to him. He replied, "Gabriel." They told him that they were enemies to Gabriel and that Michael was the angel they favored. Verses 2:97–98 respond to their statement. They do not claim that all Jews are the enemies of God. The verses clearly say that whoever is an enemy to God, his angels, or his messengers will bring upon themselves the enmity of God.

Then there is verse 9:29, which seemingly suggests that Muslims are to kill all Jews and Christians unless and until they pay a poll tax, which reflects their humiliation and subjugation. Once again, the historical and textual context of the verse in question helps explain its meaning. First of all, as we mentioned earlier, the Qur'an allows fighting only in self-defense, and thus this verse should be understood in the context of that general principle. When the Qur'an tells the believers to "fight the ones among those to whom scripture has been given," it is those Christians and/or Jews who actively fight against the Muslims. Indeed, along with the several hostile pagan Arab tribes that constantly fought against the Muslims, there were hostile Christian tribes as well. The most prominent of these was the tribe of Ghassan. The Prophet had sent two messengers to the tribe in order to invite them to become Muslims. They responded by killing the two unarmed messengers, an act of utter hostility, because messengers were never to be killed. Thus, it was clear that the Ghassan had no intention of living in peace with the Muslims.

Furthermore, the Byzantine Empire supported the tribe of Ghassan in its fight against the Prophet. This is why he sent an army of thirty thousand to the town of Tabuk to engage the Byzantine Empire. It was not to kill all Jews and Christians, in obedience to verse 9:29. Verse 9:29 tells the Prophet to fight those people of the scripture who fight him, in self-defense. Had this verse been a call to kill all Christians and Jews, the Prophet would have also attacked the Christians of Najran. He did not do so. In fact, he invited the top Christian leaders of Najran to Medina for three days of religious dialogue, hosting them in the mosque itself, and even allowing them to perform a Christian mass there. Furthermore, had 9:29 been a general exhortation to kill all Christians and Jews, the Prophet—upon signing his treaty with the Meccans at Hudaybiyah—would have dispatched his armies to attack the Christians in Byzantium, Egypt, and elsewhere. He did not. In fact, he sent the kings of various empires, including the Byzantine and Persian empires, letters inviting them to convert to Islam during the peace brought by the armistice of Hudaybiyah.

Yes, the Prophet did attack the Jewish enclave of Khaybar. But he did this because it was they who instigated the assault upon Medina by all the pagan Arab tribes; they started the hostilities against the Muslims. Thus, the Prophet was only fighting back in self-defense, as the Qur'an commands the believers to do.

In addition, verse 9:29 is the only one to speak of the *jizya*. This word comes from the verb *jaza*, which means "compensation." This *jizya*, translated as "tribute" or "exemption tax," was not imposed to humiliate non-Muslims. In an Islamic state, every able-bodied Muslim had to undergo compulsory military service, to defend the religious freedom or political safety of the people. It was a religious obligation for those Muslims. Non-Muslim citizens, however, were not obliged to serve in the military, because they were not bound by Islamic religious law. Despite this, non-Muslim citizens were given full rights of protection by the state, just like their Muslim compatriots. In addition, Muslims were required to pay *zakat*, the 2.5 percent alms tax for the poor, which the non-Muslim citizens were also not obliged to pay. Therefore, to compensate for this disparity, non-Muslim subjects would pay the *jizya*, or exemption tax. Typically, it was a sum that amounted to less than *zakat*, and in return for the *jizya*, the non-Muslim citizen would be exempt from military service. If he volunteered for military service, he would not have to pay *jizya*. Furthermore, those non-Muslim citizens who, by virtue of their status, would be automatically exempt from military service—women, males who had not yet reached maturity, elderly men, all sick or crippled men, and religious clerics—also were exempt from paying the *jizya*. Thus, far from being a tax to "humiliate" non-Muslim subjects, the *jizya* was a just and equitable system to help fund the common defense.

Far from being derogatory toward Christians and Jews, the Qur'an is, in fact, quite sophisticated in dealing with non-Muslims, especially Christians and Jews. We must remember that, when the Prophet first arrived in Medina, it was hoped that he could bring an end to the tribal clashes that were tearing the community apart. He came as a reconciler and he must have hoped that the revelation he was being given would be embraced as a unifying message. There are some verses in the Qur'an that call upon Jews and Christians to believe in the message of Muhammad: "O Children of Israel! Remember My blessing, with which I have blessed you. And I fulfill My promise; so fulfill your promise. And let it be Me that you fear. And believe in what I revealed to you, verifying what you have; and do not be the first to reject it. And do not sell My signs for a petty price; and be mindful of Me" (2:40–41). Verse 5:19 says, "People of scripture, Our messenger has come to you to make things clear for you after an intermission in the messengers, lest you say, 'No bearer of good news has come to us, and no warner.' So a bearer of good news and a warner has come to you. And God is capable of all things" (5:19).

The Qur'an praises the Torah of Moses and Gospel of Jesus several times, and this verse is but one example: "God revealed the Book to you in truth, verifying what was before it; God revealed the Torah and the Gospel before as guidance to humanity; and God revealed the Criterion [between right and wrong]" (3:3). As mentioned previously, the Qur'an highly praises a great number of the Jewish Prophets.

Of course, we know now that in addition to the pagan Arabs, some Jews and Christians embraced Muhammad's call, while many others did not. In recognition of this, the revelations began to address people at large through a "reconciling principle," al Kalimah as Sawa'. Muhammad's call was, in other words, not a call for everyone to embrace the form of religion he offered but to at least be reconciled to each other on the basis of a common understanding:

> Say: "O followers of earlier revelation! Come unto that tenet which we and you hold in common: that we shall worship none but God, and that we shall not ascribe divinity to aught beside Him, and that we shall not take human beings for our lords beside God."
>
> And if they turn away, then say: "Bear witness that it is we who have surrendered ourselves unto Him." (3:64)

There is no doubt that this is a challenging proposition for most Christians and Jews, but from the Muslim point of view the teachings of Jesus and the prophets of Israel were authentic teachings, before they were corrupted by certain later practices and theological propositions. The essential message of Islam is to call people back to utter trust and faith in God alone, not in some theology of incarnation and redemption, and certainly not in some humanly constructed dogmatic, hierarchical authority. From this point of view, reading the Gospels and the Torah a certain way would reveal a religion essentially harmonious with the revelation of the Qur'an. Therefore, Jews and Christians were challenged to live by what their own scriptures actually taught, as opposed to what various human authorities interpreted their meaning to be: "Say, 'People of scripture, you have nothing to stand on unless you live up to the Torah and the Gospel and everything sent down to you from your Lord' " (5:68). In another set of verses, the Qur'an asks: "Why don't the rabbis and religious authorities prevent their sinful talk and forbidden consumption? Evil indeed is what they've been doing" (5:63). In addition, the Qur'an declares: "And let people of the Gospel judge by what God has revealed in it. And those who do not judge by what God has revealed are the ones who are going astray" (5:47).

There is no verse among the more than six thousand verses of the Qur'an that issues a blanket condemnation of Jews and Christians. On the contrary, the Qur'an says:

> They are not [all] the same: among the people of scripture is a community that is upstanding; they read the signs of God through the hours of the night, prostrating themselves. They believe in God and the last day, and they enjoin what is fair and forbid what is repugnant, and they race to good deeds; they are among the righteous. And whatever good they do, they will not be denied it; God knows the conscientious. (3:113–115)

In fact, about Christians the Qur'an says:

> And you will certainly find the closest of them in affection to the believers are those who say, "We are Christians." That is because there are priests and monks among them, and because they are not arrogant. (5:82)

Indeed, this verse initially applied to some of the Christians in Arabia at the time of the Prophet, but it has remained applicable to this day. Moreover, there is no verse in the Qur'an that says every Christian and Jew will go to hell. On the contrary, the Qur'an says:

> The Muslims, the Jews, the Christians, and the Sabians, any who believe in God and the last day and do good have their reward with their Lord. There is nothing for them to fear; nor will they grieve. (2:62)

The guiding principle in the Qur'an with respect to non-Muslims is one of tolerance and mutual respect: "God has not forbidden you to be charitable and just to those who have not fought you over religion or driven you out from your homes, for God loves the just" (60:8). Not only does the Qur'an not declare war against the unbelievers, it also firmly rejects forced conversion: "Let there be no coercion in religion: truth stands out clear from error" (2:256). This statement is quite clear and unequivocal. Yes, the Qur'an does say, "In relation to God, religion is surrender [*islam*]" (3:19) and "If anyone seeks other than submission to God [*islam*] as a religion, it will not be accepted from him; and he will be a loser in the hereafter" (3:85). Yet, the "Islam" about which these verses speak is submitting one's will to that of God. It is the religion of all the prophets and messengers of God, as we discussed previously. In fact, the Qur'an fully acknowledges and accepts that there will be a plurality of religions on earth. It is, according to the Qur'an, part of God's will: "And had God willed, He would have made you one people: but God leaves astray whom God will. And you will surely be questioned about what you have been doing" (16:93). Furthermore, the Qur'an explains the implications of the plurality of faiths on earth:

Unto every one of you have We appointed a [different] law and way of life. And if God had so willed, He could surely have made you all one single community: but He willed it otherwise in order to test you by means of what He has vouchsafed unto you. Vie, then, with one another in doing good works! Unto God you all must return; and then He will make you truly understand all that on which you were wont to differ. (5:48)

The Austrian-born Muhammad Asad, one of the great Muslim intellectuals of the twentieth century, explains this very important passage in the following way:

The expression "every one of you" denotes the various communities of which mankind is composed. The term *shir'ah* (or *shari'ah*) signifies, literally, "the way to a watering-place" (from which men and animals derive the element indispensable to their life), and is used in the Qur'an to denote a system of law necessary for a community's social and spiritual welfare. The term *minhaj*, on the other hand, denotes an "open road," usually in an abstract sense: that is, "a way of life." The terms *shir'ah* and *minhaj* are more restricted in their meaning than the term *din*, which comprises not merely the laws relating to a particular religion but also the basic, unchanging spiritual truths which, according to the Qur'an, have been preached by every one of God's apostles, while the particular body of laws (*shir'ah* or *shari'ah*) promulgated through them, and the way of life (*minhaj*) recommended by them, varied in accordance with the exigencies of the time and of each community's cultural development. This "unity in diversity" is frequently stressed in the Qur'an (e.g., in the first sentence of 2:148, in 21:92–93, or in 23:52ff.). Because of the universal applicability and textual incorruptibility of its teachings—as well as of the fact that the Prophet Muhammad is "the seal of all prophets," i.e., the last of them (see 33:40)—the Qur'an represents the culminating point of all revelation and offers the final, perfect way to spiritual fulfillment. This uniqueness of the Qur'anic message does not, however, preclude all adherents of earlier faiths from attaining to God's grace: for—as the Qur'an so often points out—those among them who believe uncompromisingly in the One God and the Day of Judgment (i.e., in individual moral responsibility) and live righteously "need have no fear, and neither shall they grieve" [Muhammad Asad, *The Message of the Qur'an*].

Verse 5:48 is one of the most amazing verses in the entire text: the Qur'an is telling us, "God could have easily made all of you follow the same religion. That, however, is not his plan. Therefore, work together for the common good." So many of the world's problems would be solved if human beings would only heed this truly remarkable Qur'anic advice.

JIHAD

Another grossly misunderstood concept in Islam—misunderstood by both Muslims and non-Muslims alike—is that of *ji-*

had. The term *jihad* has taken on a very charged meaning in popular American culture, especially after September 11. *Jihad* is most often translated as "holy war," a term drawn from our Western Christian vocabulary. In fact, the term "holy war" does not exist in the Islamic lexicon. Some claim *jihad* is the perpetual war to convert the "abode of war" (i.e., non-Muslim areas) to the "abode of Islam." There are some Muslims who believe this as well, and there was a period in Islamic history when this was the official policy of the Muslim state, particularly during the Umayyad dynasty (680–750 C.E.). Yet some scholars suggest that the Umayyads put this policy in place in order to deflect attention away from their oppressive social policies and corrupt administration. In fact, the most famous Umayyad leader, Umar ibn Abd Al Aziz, put a stop to this policy because he knew it was unsustainable. That *jihad* means a perpetual war against non-Muslims is supported neither by the Qur'an nor the hadith.

Jihad literally means "struggle," or "striving." It is not, as some have claimed, the "sixth pillar" of Islam. *Jihad* is a very broad concept in Islam; it is an activist principle: the struggle to do good on earth for the sake of God. In the Qur'an it is a word that is distinct from *qital,* which means armed conflict. In some instances, as a last resort, *jihad* can and does encompass armed conflict. Yet armed *jihad* has very strict rules and regulations, as we discussed earlier. When used in the Qur'an, *jihad* is very general in nature, while the verses that speak about *qital* are very specific and have a number of qualifiers. For example, verse 2:190, of which we spoke earlier in detail, has very specific parameters: fighting is allowed only against those who fight the Muslims. *Jihad,* on the other hand, is much more broad:

O you who have attained to faith! Shall I point out to you
a bargain that will save you from grievous suffering [in
this world and in the life to come]?

You are to believe in God and His Apostle, and to
strive hard in God's cause with your possessions and your
lives: this is for your own good—if you but knew it!

[If you do so,] He will forgive you your sins, and will
admit you into gardens through which running waters
flow, and into goodly mansions in [those] gardens of perpetual bliss: that [will be] the triumph supreme!

And [withal, He will grant you] yet another thing that
you dearly love: succour from God [in this world], and a
victory soon to come: and [thereof, O Prophet,] give you
a glad tiding to all who believe. (61:11–13)

So, what is *jihad*, really? Is it a tangible process that can be
grasped every single day? Absolutely.

One day, during the time when the early Muslim community was struggling for its very existence, the Prophet and his
Companions had just returned from a particularly difficult battle. As they were beginning to relax, he turned to his beloved
Companions and said, "We have just returned from the lesser
jihad, but now we are entering the greater *jihad*."

"Oh Prophet of God, what do you mean?"

"I mean," he said, "that the greater *jihad* is the struggle
with our own egos." At the heart of Islamic teaching is the
idea that there is an aspect of ourselves, the *nafs*, which can
be translated variously as ego, self, or soul, that must be
brought into line with our highest understanding and intention. If this is not done, it will enslave us and lead us away
from the greater good. If we follow our selfish egoism, if we

are enslaved to a myriad of personal likes and dislikes, the reality of the Divine Presence will slip further and further from our consciousness.

The practices of Islam, the five daily prayers and the annual fast, as well as all the exhortations to moral and altruistic behavior that are the main message of the Qur'an, are there to free us from this slavery to the ego. It's not that the human self must kill every desire in order to be spiritual. In fact, the good things of life are explicitly permitted, as long as we keep them within certain lawful bounds and do not exploit others to attain them. What Islam calls for is a healthy discipline and the surrender of the self to the remembrance of God. To live this way is for most of us a constant struggle with our egoism, but this commitment to struggle is what gradually purifies the heart so that doing the good, beyond personal self-interest, becomes second nature, our spontaneous choice.

The fast of Ramadan teaches us to look beyond our immediate cravings. The times of prayer require us to disengage from the incessant, compulsive activity of our lives. The giving of charity teaches us that our wealth is not entirely our own and that generosity is actually a key to prosperity. Above all, keeping the remembrance of God in the center of our consciousness changes our perception of the meaning of life. It enables us to make greater efforts without being attached to the outcome of those efforts. "Trust in Allah, but tether your camel first," said Muhammad. Trust in God is never an excuse for becoming passive. Struggle, effort, and a humble determination are the attributes of faith.

GENDER

To begin to address all the issues of gender inequality, patriarchy, and sexual politics in the world, including the Muslim world, is not a task for a book such as this. What we can hope to do, however, is to ask the question: What is there in the primary sources of the Islamic faith (namely the Qur'an and hadith) that would justify sexism, patriarchy, or the devaluation of women? In addressing these issues we will look first at the Qur'an, and next at the sayings of the Prophet, keeping in mind that these sayings, though held in the greatest respect, cannot be verified 100 percent individually. Therefore, if a hadith of Muhammad's inspires and guides us, and it is consistent with the Qur'an, we are on safe ground. If a hadith, however, adds something of a legal nature that is not found in the Qur'an, or even possibly seems to contradict it, we have a right to be cautious. We believe it will be clear from the issues discussed below that the Qur'an shows womankind in a positive light and grants equal rights to women. In fact, it is on the basis of the Qur'an that the struggle for the attainment of women's rights in Islamic societies is proceeding. There are serious issues to be confronted and we are living through a time of reevaluation, reinterpretation, and reconciliation.

Somehow the notion that in Islam women are not treated fairly has become a widespread belief. Through the media we pick up bits and pieces of information—the Taliban forbid women's education; the Saudis won't let women drive or vote; police in Iran patrol the streets looking for couples holding hands, and so forth. The example of certain hard-line Islamic societies presents a picture of women covered from head to toe and facing all kinds of restrictions in public life. This certainly does not give a favorable impression of Islam. The fundamental question to be answered is: Are these conditions somehow intrinsic to Islam, or are they part of the cultural baggage of particular societies? Is this the direction in which Islam inevitably leads, or one possible expression of it, or a deviation from Islam's principles?

> And the faithful, both men and women—they are close unto one another: they enjoin the doing of what is right and forbid the doing of what is wrong, and are constant in prayer, and give in purifying charity, and pay heed unto God and His Prophet. It is they upon whom God will bestow His grace: verily, God is almighty, wise! (9:71)

The word rendered as "close unto one another," *awliya,* can also mean friends or protectors. It is also the word used for saints, or the "friends" of God. *Awliya* (plural of *wali*) is packed with beautiful associations. Imagine men and women who see each other as intimate friends. Or imagine a relationship of saints married to each other. And to take it one step further, the verse mentioned above does not even say "married men and women," but the faithful, the believers, those living a spiritual life. This is the ideal within Islam, which has somehow become distorted in the minds of some into a patriarchal relationship of dominance. And yet within the religion itself is the key to unlock the prison of patriarchy. The above verse is followed by this one:

> God has promised the believers, both men and women, gardens through which running waters flow, therein to abide, and goodly dwellings in gardens of perpetual bliss: but God's goodly acceptance is the greatest [bliss of all]—for this, this is the triumph supreme! (9:72)

So are these gardens of perpetual bliss a reward of the afterlife, or . . . ? The Qur'an wisely and profoundly leaves this an open question. The Prophet Muhammad once said, "Marriage [i.e., a good one] amounts to half of the religion." What is clear from all the primary sources is that Islam respects and sanctifies human sexuality. From the perspective of Islam, sexuality, when approached in the context of a committed and respectful relationship, is a positive support to the spiritual life. It is a gift ordained by God.

> They are as a garment for you, and you are as a garment
> for them . . . Now, then, you may lie with them skin to
> skin, and avail yourselves of that which God has ordained
> for you. (2:187)

That being said, we can now look at some of the gender-related misconceptions that have been promulgated about Islam.

Polygamy

One of the most controversial associations with Islam in the minds of many people is polygamy. In the wild imaginings fueled by cinematic clichés, it conjures up images of harems arranged for the sexual gratification of portly patriarchs. At the very least it transgresses something of a moral absolute in the mind of modern Westerners: one woman for one man. In our minds we compare the monogamous ideal that we imagine is the norm for our societies with sordid images of women deprived of free will and treated as sexual objects. In doing so, we conveniently overlook the extent of sexual objectification, spousal abuse, adultery, and rape rampant within Western societies. We compare our own highest ideal with a degraded stereotype. People in Middle Eastern societies play the same game, imagining that the West is a playground of free love. Cultures judge each other on the basis of externals and superficialities. One side condemns the other for the amount of cloth women do or don't wear.

At the time that the Qur'an was revealed, women had few rights in Arabian tribal society. The verse that allowed marriage to more than one wife was addressing the problem of orphaned women who might otherwise be merely maintained as servants, or whose assets might be mismanaged by their guardians. Instead, it proposed that marriage be offered to them to legitimize their status, but it placed clear responsibilities on the husband: "Marry women who please you, two, three, or four; but if you fear you won't be equitable, then [marry] one" (4:3).

First of all, polygamy is nothing new; it has been practiced since the very beginnings of human history. Islam did not invent the practice. In fact, King Solomon had dozens of wives and concubines, as the Bible clearly mentions. Yet, more importantly, Islamic law is very strict when it comes to taking on another wife, assuming, of course, one's current wife acquiesces to her husband taking on a second wife. If she does not like the idea of sharing her husband, then she has the right to ask for a divorce. In fact, the woman can stipulate in the marriage contract that her husband cannot take a second wife.

Furthermore, the latter part of the verse quoted above is extremely important, and frequently neglected by proponents of polygamy: "but if you fear you won't be equitable, then [marry] one." Thus, the most important thing is justice between wives: all wives must have equal status, separate and equivalent houses and possessions, and so forth. If a judge in an Islamic court deems that a man cannot be just to all of his wives, he can prevent him from marrying more than one wife.

From a sociological perspective, polygamy may make sense in certain situations when it solves acute societal problems. For instance, in the aftermath of war, typically many of the men are killed, and women make up a majority of those left alive. If the male is the main breadwinner for families, polygamy may serve to reduce the problem of women left without a means of support.

The Qur'an does not order men to marry more than one wife; it merely allows for the possibility. In fact, the Qur'an makes an important statement regarding justice between wives: "You will not be able to treat women the same, no matter how hard you try; but do not be completely partial, so as to leave a woman in suspense. And if you reconcile and are conscientious, God is most forgiving, most merciful" (4:129). Many commentators suggest that this verse indicates that monogamy is the preferred marital arrangement.

The volume of self-righteous condemnation regarding the Qur'anic acceptance of polygamy is interesting considering that there is a de facto widespread "polygamy" practiced in the West, where several polls suggest that as many as 70 percent of married men, and close to 60 percent of married women, have admitted to committing adultery. If a Muslim man takes a second wife—and pledges to love, honor, and care for her—he is viewed as "barbaric" if not "immoral." Yet the cries of condemnation are not nearly as loud when a married man commits adultery, threatening to destroy his family, which is the foundation of our society, nor when a man divorces a wife of many years and marries a younger one.

Nevertheless, the controversy over polygamy has truly been

overblown, particularly in the West. Polygamy has been made illegal in the majority of Muslim countries today. In addition, the overwhelming majority of Muslim men have only one wife and are content with having only one wife. Rather than being the norm, polygamy among Muslims is the exception.

Muhammad and His Wives

Muhammad was a model husband. He regularly did work around the house—sweeping, cleaning, mending sandals—and was a delight to his wives. His first marriage, which lasted for many years—to a very independent woman perhaps fifteen years his senior—was a model of monogamous happiness. Only after Khadija passed away did he take on more than one wife, some of them being widows or previously divorced women, these relationships often establishing positive kinship bonds with various tribes. None of his wives were coerced to marry; all were free to divorce him; and none of them made that choice.

One of the most heinous accusations against the Prophet Muhammad is the accusation that he was a pedophile. This stems from the fact that his beloved wife, Aisha, was betrothed to him while she was still a child—perhaps nine years old. We do not know for sure when the marriage was consummated, but we do know that nothing about this arrangement was considered immoral or unusual by the society of the day. The suggestion that there was something exploitive or abusive in this relationship has no basis whatever. Abu Bakr, the father of Aisha, was one of the most respected members of the Meccan community, a lifelong companion of Muhammad's, and the man chosen by the community to be Caliph after Muhammad's death. The child bride in question, Aisha, remained the adoring, though sometimes impetuous, wife of the Prophet and grew into a figure of great stature, wisdom, and authority.

The Verse About "Striking"

Perhaps one of the most controversial verses of the Qur'an is one that seems to sanction a husband striking his wife. Here is the verse:

> As for those of whom you have reason to fear flagrant immoral behavior [harming themselves or others], at first admonish them; next separate yourselves from them [literally: "leave them alone in bed"]; and [only as a last resort] strike them [lightly]. And if they obey you, then seek no means against them. For God is exalted, great. (4:34)

There are many women and men—Muslims among them—who might find this a challenging or disturbing proposition. It is even said that Muhammad was not entirely comfortable with it and commented, "I wished for it to be otherwise but Allah wished it so." We honestly feel that a discussion of this verse should not be avoided, and we hope to shed some light on how this verse has been interpreted historically by the majority of Muslim legal scholars. In no way, shape, or form, however, do we justify, condone, or accept any act of violence toward anyone, be it from within or from outside a bond of marriage. Nevertheless, however one may finally feel about this, the verse does exist, and there are certain things that can be said to put this into context.

First, let us examine the attitude of the Qur'an toward marriage and spousal relations. The overwhelming themes stressed are love, mercy, compassion, and mutual partnership: "Among the signs of God is having created mates for you from yourselves that you may feel at home with them, creating love and compassion between you. Surely there are signs in that for people who reflect" (30:21). In this verse, the Arabic word for "signs" can also mean "miracle," and thus one of God's miracles is that he created mates and spouses with whom we dwell in tranquility, and he put between the spouses love and mercy. In another verse previously mentioned, God says: "They are your garments and you are their garments" (2:187). The use of the term "garments" is quite interesting. A garment is something that covers one's body, keeps it warm from the cold, and protects it from the rain and snow. A garment is the closest thing to the body, and it can be used for adornment as well. The same can be said of the spouse: he or she is close, covers up one's faults, and keeps one warm and protected. It is a very intimate and compassionate description, and it connotes a close and intimate relationship between husband and wife. The relationship between man and wife, according to the Qur'an, should be one of harmony, balance, and intimacy.

Second, it is extremely important to point out that the Prophet never once used physical force with any of his wives. Never. In fact, even when his wives upset him, he chose to isolate himself from them, living alone for a short period of time. The following verses of the Qur'an transmit God's revelation regarding the Prophet's wives: "O Prophet, say to your wives, 'If you desire the life of the world and its finery, come then and I will provide for you, and divorce you on the best of terms. But if you want God and God's prophet, and the home of the hereafter, God has prepared a tremendous reward for those of you who do good'" (33:28–29). In addition, the Prophet was very clear that wives are not to be beaten, and he abhorred any violence against women. He said on more than one occasion, "Could any of you beat his wife as he would beat a slave, and then lie with her in the evening?" Another time, the Prophet said, "Never beat God's handmaidens."

Still, we are faced with verse 4:34, which authorizes husbands to strike their wives. Those who seek to malign Islam selectively quote the very end of the verse to claim the Qur'an advocates "wife-beating." When examined in toto, however, verse 4:34 clearly sets out to outline how to resolve the problem of severe disruption of marital harmony. The first thing the verse advocates is admonition: talking out the problem; trying to settle the issue through communication. If this fails, the next step is not violence, which might have been a natural next step for the Arab man at the time of the Prophet (and sometimes even today, unfortunately), but separation: "leave them alone in bed." This is a "cooling-off" period during which each partner can think about the problem at hand. If this does not work and severe discord continues, only then is the possibility of some physical action permitted. But this is not at all a command to beat them into submission.

Traditional authorities are virtually unanimous in asserting that this "striking" should be symbolic in nature and should be done only as an absolute last resort if the wife, according to the Prophet, "has become guilty, in an obvious manner, of immoral conduct." Also, the Prophet stressed that it should not cause any pain; again, it should be a symbolic "nudge." Some preeminent classical Muslim scholars, such as Al-Shafi'i, believed that the command to "strike them" was barely permissible and should preferably be avoided. More modern scholars, such as Ibn Ashour, maintain that despite the verse's authorization of

striking the wife, Muslim judges are empowered to prohibit
husbands from laying hands on their wives at all, especially if
application of this verse would lead to more harm than good.
We believe this would be the case today, given the major problem of domestic violence in some modern societies. Moreover,
the authorization to "strike" the wife in verse 4:34 is similar to
the story of Job in Islamic tradition. Job, when his wife had
complained about their desolation, became angry with his wife
and vowed to strike her one hundred times for her ingratitude
to God. After God restored his health and strength, an angel
came to Job with one hundred tiny branches and told him,
"Strike this lightly on your wife, and you will have fulfilled your
vow." When understood in the context of Arabian society at
the time of the Prophet, verse 4:34 is a prescription for moder-
ation.

At the time of the Prophet, women were treated as property,
and they were frequently maltreated and beaten. In fact, female infants were murdered in pre-Islamic Arabian society,
which the Qur'an strongly condemns: by declaring that, on
Judgment Day, God will ask "the infant girl who was buried
[alive] . . . for what offense she was killed" (81:8–9). Verse 4:34
is teaching husbands that the first step in resolving marital
problems is not violence but mutual discussion and reasoning.
That is the preferred method of the Qur'an in resolving marital differences, and verse 4:128 echoes the same sentiment, this
time in case of cruelty on the part of the husband: "If a woman
fears abuse or desertion from her husband, there is no blame on
them if they find a compromise between them. And compromise is best, though avarice draws souls. If you act kindly and
are conscientious, God is aware of what you do." Notice that it

says "compromise is best." Not violence, not harsh treatment, not forcing women into submission, but amicable settlement.

Inheritance and Testimony

There are other verses in the Qur'an that have been taken by both Muslims and non-Muslims to mean that women are inferior to men. In verse 2:282, the Qur'an speaks about witnesses to a financial contract: "And get the testimony of two witnesses from your men; or if there are not two men, then a man and two women of your choice from among the witnesses, so that if one of them errs [is led astray] the other may remind her." There are those who have taken this verse to mean that the testimony of a woman is only worth half that of a man. This is not, however, a valid conclusion. First of all, this verse is the only one that specifies that two men or one man and two women should be chosen as witnesses. In all other verses that call for witnesses, the term is general, without specification as to the gender: "Then when you turn their property over to them, have it witnessed for them, though God is sufficient in accounting" (4:6); "If any of your women are guilty of lewdness, call for evidence against them from four of you" (4:15); and "Believers, when death comes to one of you, let there be witnesses among you at the time of the legacy, by two just individuals from among you, or two others from different people if a fatal calamity befalls you while you are traveling the earth" (5:106). Thus, only verse 2:282 specifies the gender of the witnesses. This is because women at the time of the Prophet were, in general, not as well versed in financial affairs as men.

In addition, as the Arabian society before Islam had a long history of being harshly patriarchal, women could be coerced into bearing false witness by another man. Thus, in order to prevent injustice in financial dealings, the Qur'an specifies two female witnesses if two men can't be found. The reason for two female witnesses is, as the Arabic text literally says, "If she is led astray, then the other can remind her." The female witness can be "led astray" by a man who wishes to pressure her to bear false witness. Two female witnesses, however, can stand up against the possible pressure from that man. The command of verse 2:282 cannot be taken as a general rule that a woman's testimony is only half as reliable as a man's. Further supporting this view is the fact that there were numerous female judges in Islamic history but no requirement that another woman had to uphold their rulings. In addition, numerous traditions of the Prophet were transmitted by women Companions, also without requiring another woman's testimony for verification. In fact, hundreds of traditions were transmitted solely from the Prophet's wife Aisha. No one demanded that another woman confirm her sayings.

Similarly, the Qur'an specifies that the share of inheritance for men is double that for women: "God directs you in regard to your children: the male gets the equivalent of the portion of two females" (4:11). Again, this may incorrectly be seen as "evidence" that the Qur'an considers women inferior to men. First of all, Islam was one of the first societies to allow inheritance by a woman at all. More importantly, however, whatever wealth a woman gets—from her business, inheritance, or other sources—is solely for her. If she is married, she has absolutely no obligation to share any of that wealth, even if it numbers in the billions of dollars, with her husband. Yet a male is responsible for his wife, children, and perhaps his mother and sisters, and if he gets any inheritance, he must use that wealth to take care of and maintain his family. Thus, men are given more in inheritance because their financial responsibilities are much more than those of women. The Qur'an regards men and women as equal: "And if any do good deeds, whether they are male or female, and they are believers, then they will enter the Garden, and will not be mistreated at all" (4:124). Another verse puts the equality of men and women in more eloquent terms:

> For the men who acquiesce to the will of God, and the women who acquiesce, the men who believe and the women who believe, the men who are devout and the women who are devout, the men who are truthful and the women who are truthful, the men who are constant and the women who are constant, the men who are humble and the women who are humble, the men who give charity and the women who give charity, the men who fast and the women who fast, the men who are chaste and the women who are chaste, and the men and women who remember God abundantly, God has arranged forgiveness for them, and a magnificent reward. (33:35)

While asserting their equality, the Qur'an is still very cognizant of the very obvious differences between men and women: "And the male is not like the female" (3:36). This does not mean that one is better than the other; it simply states a fact of nature: men and women are different. Still, the Qur'an—and by extension Islam—treats them equally.

CONCLUSION

Islam is many things to many people. For one-fifth of the world's population, it is the primary source of spiritual strength and succor. For some, particularly here in the West, Islam is a "wicked, evil" religion that espouses violence against non-Muslims and seeks to oppress women. To support their claims, they distort Islamic sacred history, and misquote or mistranslate the Qur'an or quote it completely out of context. Careful study of the Qur'an—in its proper historical, linguistic, and textual context—clearly shows, however, that it does not endorse violence or perpetual war against those who are not Muslim. Careful study of the Qur'an reveals that it endorses equality between men and women. Anyone with sinister intentions can quote a verse of scripture out of context to seemingly prove a point. That said, however, it would be extremely disingenuous of us to deny the existence of Muslims who, in fact, do claim the Qur'an calls for the murder of non-Muslims. These Muslims do, in fact, use verses such as 9:5 and 2:193 as justification for the murder of innocent people. And they do disparage Jews and Christians based upon a complete misunderstanding of Qur'anic scripture. They do claim women are inferior to men based on a completely incorrect reading of Qur'anic verses. They do commit acts of abuse against their wives because they claim the Qur'an says it is permissible to "beat them." Fortunately, they are a tiny minority of the entire Muslim world. Their actions are an affront to the principles of Islam, and they violate both the letter and the spirit of the faith. Still, the whole must never be judged by the sins of the few.

ABROGATION

If so much of the Qur'an can be shown to advocate a pluralis-
tic, even universal, spirituality, how do we explain the extreme
intolerance and narrowness of some interpretations of Islam?
The answer lies in a belief held by some—especially Ibn
Taymiyya and Ibn Kathir—that certain verses of the Qur'an
have been abrogated, or superseded, by others. Those who hold
this view take some of the verses we have already discussed, remove them from their context, interpret them in an absolutis-
tic way, and, furthermore, claim that other Qur'anic verses that
would clearly contradict their narrow and distorted interpretations have been abrogated. The justification for abrogation is
this verse:

> Any message which We annul or consign to oblivion We
> replace with a better or a similar one. Dost you not know
> that God has the power to will anything? (2:106)

This verse occurs in the middle of a passage addressing some
of those people mentioned in earlier revelations who strongly
opposed the Muslims, primarily Christians and Jews, who
wanted to hold exclusively to their own scriptures and refused
to accept that the Qur'an could have been a legitimate bestowal
from God. The verse immediately preceding this one says:

> Neither those from among the followers of earlier revela-
> tion who are bent on denying the truth, nor those who
> ascribe divinity to other beings beside God, would like to
> see any good ever bestowed upon you from on high by
> your Sustainer; but God singles out for His grace whom

He wills—for God is limitless in His great bounty.
(2:105)

Because the same word, *ayat,* is used for verses of the Qur'an
as well as the messages of earlier revelations, the abrogationists
would contend that God had reason to arbitrarily change revealed spiritual principles—to essentially rewrite the revelation
as he went along. However, there are no hadith that support
this idea, nor do the upholders of this theory of abrogation
agree among themselves as to which verses should be abrogated. It has, instead, become a convenient rationale for
distorting, or virtually amputating, parts of the Qur'an that
contradict one's own narrow agenda.

In the minds of those who uphold this "theory of abrogation," the universal message of the Qur'an has become a divi-
sive sectarian message, pitting Islam against all other faiths and
denying such universal affirmations as this:

> And indeed, within every community have We raised up
> an apostle [entrusted with this message]: "Worship God,
> and shun the powers of evil!" And among those past gen-
> erations were people whom God graced with His guid-
> ance, and some who inevitably fell prey to grievous error:
> go, then, about the earth and behold what happened in
> the end to those who gave the lie to the truth! (16:36)
> [see also 10:47, 14:4]

Such people restrict the meaning of a *mu'min* (a believer; more
literally "a faithful person") to Muslims only. Furthermore, they
have reduced the idea of a Muslim from one who is in a state

of surrender to the Divine to one who explicitly and exclusively accepts their idea of Islam, labeling not only people of all other faiths as "unbelievers," but those Muslims who disagree with them as well. Some Muslim theologians have preached that the verse that says, "Slay them wherever you find them" abrogate over 190 verses in the Qur'an that refer to the diversity of humanity, the good to be found in other religions, the primacy of virtue regardless of beliefs, and freedom of religion. Those who have used the theory of abrogation to promote an intolerant, sectarian notion of Islam have stifled interfaith dialogue, impoverished their own understanding, contributed to the fragmentation of humanity, impeded the resolution of global problems, and betrayed the merciful and generous spirit of Islam. Once again, those who hold to the idea of abrogation, though quite vocal at times, are fortunately a small minority of the Muslim faithful.

THE FATIHA

Finally, we turn to the most commonly recited prayer in Islam, the Fatiha, or "opening." It is said to contain the whole essential teaching of Islam in a few short verses. More than any other formulation, it is a reminder that orients the Muslim toward his or her essential relationship with God. It could be recited by any Christian or Jew without contradicting the essential beliefs of either tradition. If analyzed, it is remarkably close in structure to the Lord's Prayer of Christianity, in that its first few verses are praise of the Divine and its last verses ask for guidance and support. Here it is:

In the name of God, the Infinitely Compassionate and Merciful.
All praise is God's, the Sustainer of the universes,
The Infinitely Compassionate and Merciful, Ruler on the Day of
    Reckoning.
You alone do we worship and You alone do we ask for help.
Guide us on the straight path,
The path of those who have received your Grace,
Not the path of those who have incurred wrath,
Nor of those who wander astray.
Amen.

APPENDIX I

SUGGESTED READING LIST

Armstrong, Karen. *Islam: A Short History*. New York: Modern Library, 2002.

Asad, Muhammad. *The Message of the Qur'an*. Bristol, UK: The Book Foundation, 2003.

Lings, Martin. *Muhammad: His Life Based on the Earliest Sources*. Rochester, VT: Inner Traditions, 1987.

Murata, Sachiko, and William Chittick. *The Vision of Islam*. St. Paul, MN: Paragon House Publishers, 1995.

Nasr, Seyyed Hossein. *The Heart of Islam: Enduring Values for Humanity*. New York: HarperCollins, 2002.

Rauf, Feisal Abdul. *What's Right with Islam Is What's Right with America: A New Vision for Muslims and the West*. San Francisco: HarperSanFrancisco, 2005.

Siddiqi, Muhammad Zubayr. *Hadith Literature: Its Origin, Development, and Special Features*. Cambridge, UK: Islamic Texts Society, 1996.

Yusuf, Hamza (translator), and Shaykh Al-Amin Ali Mazrui (collector). *The Content of Character: Ethical Sayings of the Prophet Muhammad*. Cambridge, UK: Sandala, 2005.

GLOSSARY OF KEY TERMS

Allah: God. Although understood by some as a different God, "Allah" is the Arabic equivalent of the names for God used in the Bible.

Gabriel: The chief of the archangels, who, according to Muslims, is charged with carrying revelation from God to the prophets. Muslims believe Gabriel was sent to Abraham, Moses, and Jesus, among other prophets.

hadith: Literally, "news" or "speech," denoting the sayings of the Prophet Muhammad. The hadith are generally accepted by Muslims as a secondary source of Islamic law.

Hajj: The once-in-a-lifetime pilgrimage to Mecca that is incumbent upon those Muslims physically and financially able to make it. It consists of a series of rituals that reenact the ancient story of Abraham, Hagar, and Ishmael in the wilderness of Paran.

Iblis: Arabic name for the devil.

ihsan: Righteousness based on a deep sense of what is both good and beautiful. Portrayed by the Prophet Muhammad as living and acting as if you see God right in front of you and, if you don't, knowing that you are seen by God.

iman: Commonly translated as "faith," *iman* is a certainty of the heart about the beneficence and order of the universe—in other words, the recognition that we live in a spiritual reality.

Insha'Allah: "God willing." Muslims frequently append this phrase at the end of a sentence declaring an intention to do something in the future.

islam: Literally, "submission." The name for the religion of the Prophet Muhammad.

Jahannam: The Arabic name for hell.

jihad: Struggle; taken to mean "holy war" by many people, especially in the West. *Jihad,* however, does not mean "holy war," but rather the struggle to live one's life according to the divine will.

Ka'ba: The central shrine of Islam, the place Muslims face to make their ritual prayers. Muslims believe the shrine was originally built by the Prophet Abraham and his son Ishmael for the worship of the One God.

kafir: A common Arabic term for unbelievers, used by some in a derogatory manner. However, *kafir* actually means "one who conceals or covers up." Thus, a *kafir* is anyone who denies or refuses to acknowledge the truth.

Khadija: Wealthy woman merchant who married the Prophet Muhammad before his ministry began. She was his only wife for more than twenty years. She bore the Prophet two sons, who died in childhood, and four daughters, who all lived to see their father become a prophet.

kufr: Literally means "denial." Commonly mistranslated as "nonbelief," it is the willful denial of the spiritual dimension of life to follow the impulses of the ego instead.

Mecca: The city, located in modern-day Saudi Arabia, in which the Prophet Muhammad was born in 570 C.E. He was expelled from Mecca in 623, and he later conquered it in 630. Mecca houses the central shrine of Islam, the Ka'ba, which Muslims face to make their five daily ritual prayers.

Medina: A city three hundred miles to the north of Mecca where the Prophet Muhammad migrated after being expelled from Mecca. Originally called Yathrib, it was renamed Madinat-un-Nabi, or "City of the Prophet," from which the name "Medina" comes. The Prophet's mosque and tomb is located in Medina.

Muhammad: The seventh-century Arabian merchant who is believed to be the Last Prophet of God by Muslims.

People of the Book: The term that the Qur'an uses to describe Jews and Christians.

qadr: Destiny, understood by Muslims to mean the divine decree of God.

qital: Fighting. Fighting in Islam is allowed only in self-defense and as a last resort, and it has very specific rules and restrictions as outlined by the Qur'an and the sayings of the Prophet Muhammad. *Qital* is a concept distinct from *jihad,* or the struggle to live in accordance with the divine will.

Qur'an: Islam's revealed sacred text. Qur'an literally means "recitation" in Arabic.

Quraysh: The tribe of the Prophet Muhammad.

Ramadan: The ninth month in the Islamic calendar. During this month, Muslims abstain from food, drink, and other sensual pleasures from dawn until dusk. Muslims also believe the Qur'an was first revealed to the Prophet Muhammad during Ramadan.

Sahih Bukhari: The most famous collection of hadith, or sayings of the Prophet Muhammad. The collection of Bukhari is considered by most Muslims to be second only to the Qur'an in authority. The collection was named after Imam Bukhari, a Persian scholar.

Sahih Muslim: The second most famous collection of hadith, believed to be as authentic as the collection of Bukhari. Sahih Muslim was named after Imam Muslim, a scholar of the Arab tribe Qushayr.

salah: The five daily ritual prayers that must be performed by Muslims.

shahadah: The Muslim testimony of faith. It reads: "There is nothing worthy of worship except God, and Muhammad is His Messenger." This statement is typically read publicly if someone wishes to convert to Islam.

Shariah: An Arabic term meaning "way" or "path," the Shariah is the body of Islamic law derived from the Qur'an and hadith of the Prophet Muhammad.

Shaytan: Satan.

Shi'ism: Its origins lie in a dispute about the true significance and authority of Imam Ali, who became the fourth Caliph after Muhammad. Following Ali's assassination, his descendants maintained a kind of spiritual dynasty, claiming spiritual authority in the name of the family of the Prophet. Gradually certain practices developed that distinguished the Shi'as in relatively minor ways from the majority Sunnis.

siyam: Fasting.

Sufism: Derived from the word *tassawuf,* which means "purification," Sufism is a voluntary spiritual education under the guidance of a shaikh and following one of numerous *tariqas,* or paths, established by various Pirs, or founders, such as, Rumi, Abdul Qadir Gilani, and Ahmed Rufai. Many of Islam's greatest leaders, scholars, poets, and jurists have been associated with and influenced by Sufism.

Sunnah: Arabic for "way" or "manner." The Sunnah is the tradition of the Prophet Muhammad, as distinct from the actual sayings of the Prophet.

Sunni Islam: The largest of the two primary divisions within Islam. Sunni orthodoxy was established on the basis of the Qur'an, the Sunnah (example and practice) of the Prophet Muhammad, and also through a general consensus that took clear shape by the third Islamic century (approximately 900 C.E.). Accounting for about 80 percent of Muslims, it was gradually established in polarity with Shi'ism, the minority branch.

taqwa: Guarding oneself from the negative effects of one's own heedlessness.

zakat: The annual alms tax due from the Muslim faithful. It amounts to 2.5 percent of all unused excess wealth saved up for one year.

570 The birth of Prophet Muhammad.

595 The Prophet's marriage to Khadija.

610 The Prophet Muhammad is first visited by the archangel Gabriel. The first verses of the Qur'an are revealed, and the mission of the Prophet begins.

618 General boycott of the Prophet and his people begins in Mecca.

621 Boycott is ended. Muhammad's wife, Khadija, and uncle, Abu Talib, die as a result of the boycott.

621 The famous night journey occurs in this year.

623 The Prophet migrates to Medina and establishes the first Islamic city-state. The Muslim calendar begins with this event.

624 The Battle of Badr.

626 The Battle of Uhud.

627 The Battle of the Trench.

628 The Treaty of Hudaybiyah.

630 The conquest of Mecca.

632 The Prophet dies in Medina. His longtime Companion Abu

Bakr is elected first Caliph of the new Muslim state. The wars of rebellion begin.

634 Abu Bakr dies. Umar, the Prophet's other closest Companion, is elected second Caliph. Massive territorial expansion of the Muslim state begins during Umar's reign. Persia is defeated, and Jerusalem is conquered.

644 Umar is assassinated by a Persian slave. Uthman ibn Affan, the Prophet's son-in-law, is elected third Caliph. Territorial expansion continues.

656 Uthman is assassinated by rebels. A dispute arises over what to do about the assassination and who is the rightful Caliph. A major civil war breaks out with two people, Ali (the Prophet's son-in-law) and Mu'awiyah ibn Abu Sufyan, claiming to be Caliph. Ali eventually wins the war.

661 Ali is assassinated in Iraq, and the Umayyad dynasty begins.

THE CONSTITUTION OF THE ISLAMIC
REPUBLIC OF MEDINA

1. This is a document from Muhammad the Prophet (may Allah bless him and grant him peace), governing relations between the Believers, i.e., Muslims of Quraysh and Yathrib, and those who followed them and worked hard with them. They form one nation—Ummah.

2. The Quraysh Mohajireen will continue to pay blood money, according to their present custom.

3. In case of war with anybody they will redeem their prisoners with kindness and justice common among Believers. [Not according to the traditions of pre-Islamic nations, where the rich and the poor were treated differently.]

4. The Bani Awf will decide the blood money, among themselves, according to their existing custom.

5. In case of war with anybody all parties other than Muslims will redeem their prisoners with kindness and justice according to practice among Believers and not in accordance with pre-Islamic notions.

6. The Bani Saeeda, the Bani Harith, the Bani Jusham, and the Bani Najjar will be governed along the lines of the above [principles].

7. The Bani Amr, Bani Awf, Bani Al-Nabeet, and Bani Al-Aws will be governed in the same manner.

8. Believers will not fail to redeem their prisoners; they will pay blood money on their behalf. It will be a common responsibility of the Ummat and not of the family of the prisoners to pay blood money.

9. A Believer will not make the freedman of another Believer his ally against the wishes of the other Believers.

10. The Believers, who fear Allah, will oppose the rebellious elements and those that encourage injustice or sin, or enmity, or corruption among Believers.

11. If anyone is guilty of any such act all the Believers will oppose him even if he be the son of any one of them.

12. A Believer will not kill another Believer for the sake of an un-Believer [i.e., even if the un-Believer is his close relative].

13. No Believer will help an un-Believer against a Believer.

14. Protection [when given] in the Name of Allah will be common. The weakest among Believers may give protection [in the name of Allah] and it will be binding on all Believers.

15. Believers are all friends to each other to the exclusion of all others.

16. Those Jews who follow the Believers will be helped and will be treated with equality. [Social, legal, and economic equality is promised to all loyal citizens of the state.]

17. No Jew will be wronged for being a Jew.

18. The enemies of the Jews who follow us will not be helped.

19. The peace of the Believers [of the state of Madinah] cannot be divided. [It is either peace or war for all. It cannot be that a part of the population is at war with the outsiders and a part is at peace.]

20. No separate peace will be made by anyone in Madinah when Believers are fighting in the Path of Allah.

21. Conditions of peace and war and the accompanying ease or hardships must be fair and equitable to all citizens alike.

22. In every foray a rider must take another behind him.

23. The Believers must avenge the blood of one another when fighting in the Path of Allah. [This clause was to remind those in front of whom there may have been less severe fighting that the cause was common to all. It also meant that although each battle appeared a separate entity it was in fact a part of the war, which affected all Muslims equally.]

24. The Believers (because they fear Allah) are better in showing steadfastness and as a result receive guidance from Allah in this respect. Others must also aspire to come up to the same standard of steadfastness.

25. No un-Believer will be permitted to take the property of the Quraysh [the enemy] under his protection. Enemy property must be surrendered to the State.

26. No un-Believer will intervene in favor of a Quraysh [because the Quraysh, having declared war, are the enemy].

27. If any un-Believer kills a Believer, without good cause, he shall be killed in return, unless the next of kin are satisfied [as killing creates law-and-order problems and weakens the defence of the state]. All Believers shall be against such a wrong-doer. No Believer will be allowed to shelter such a man.

28. When you differ on anything [regarding this document] the matter shall be referred to Allah and Muhammad [may Allah bless him and grant him peace].

29. The Jews will contribute toward the war when fighting alongside the Believers.

30. The Jews of Bani Awf will be treated as one community with the Believers. The Jews have their religion. This will also apply to their freedmen. The exception will be those who act unjustly and sinfully. By so doing they wrong themselves and their families.

31. The same applies to Jews of Bani Al-Najjar, Bani Al Harith, Bani

Saeeda, Bani Jusham, Bani Al Aws, Thaalba, and the Jaffna [a clan of the Bani Thaalba] and the Bani Al Shutayba.

32. Loyalty gives protection against treachery. [Loyal people are protected by their friends against treachery. As long as a person remains loyal to the state he is not likely to succumb to the ideas of being treacherous. He protects himself against weakness.]

33. The freedmen of Thaalba will be afforded the same status as [Thaalbans] themselves. This status is for fair dealings and full justice as a right and equal responsibility for military service.

34. Those in alliance with the Jews will be given the same treatment as the Jews.

35. No one [no tribe which is party to the pact] shall go to war except with the permission of Muhammed (may Allah bless him and grant him peace). If any wrong has been done to any person or party it may be avenged.

36. Anyone who kills another without warning [there being no just cause for it] amounts to his slaying himself and his household, unless the killing was done due to a wrong being done to him.

37. The Jews must bear their own expenses [in war] and the Muslims bear their expenses.

38. If anyone attacks anyone who is a party to this Pact the other must come to his help.

39. They [parties to this pact] must seek mutual advice and consultation.

40. Loyalty gives protection against treachery. Those who avoid mutual consultation do so because of lack of sincerity and loyalty.

41. A man will not be made liable for misdeeds of his ally.

42. Anyone [any individual or party] who is wronged must be helped.

43. The Jews must pay [for war] with the Muslims. [This clause appears to be for occasions when Jews are not taking part in the war. Clause 37 deals with occasions when they are taking part in war.]

44. Yathrib will be [a] Sanctuary for the people of this Pact.

45. A stranger [individual] who has been given protection [by anyone party to this pact] will be treated as his host [who has given him protection] while [he is] doing no harm and is not committing any crime. Those given protection but indulging in anti-state activities will be liable to punishment.

46. A woman will be given protection only with the consent of her family [guardian]. [A precaution to avoid intertribal conflicts.]

47. In case of any dispute or controversy which may result in trouble the matter must be referred to Allah and Muhammad (may Allah bless him and grant him peace), The Prophet (may Allah bless him and grant him peace) of Allah will accept anything in this document, which is for (bringing about) piety and goodness.

48. Quraysh and their allies will not be given protection.

49. The parties to this Pact are bound to help each other in the event of an attack on Yathrib.

50. If they [the parties to the pact other than the Muslims] are called upon to make and maintain peace [within the state] they must do so. If a similar demand [to make and maintain peace] is made of the Muslims, it must be carried out, except when the Muslims are already engaged in a war in the Path of Allah. [This way no secret ally of the enemy can aid the enemy by calling upon Muslims to end hostilities under this clause.]

51. Everyone [every individual] will have his share [be treated] in accordance with what party he belongs to. Individuals must benefit or suffer for the good or bad deed of the group they belong to. Without such a rule party affiliations and discipline cannot be maintained.

52. The Jews of al-Aws, including their freedmen, have the same standing as other parties to the Pact, as long as they are loyal to the Pact. Loyalty is a protection against treachery.

53. Anyone who acts loyally or otherwise does it for his own good [or loss].

54. Allah approves this Document.

55. This document will not [be employed to] protect one who is unjust or commits a crime [against other parties to the pact].

56. Whether an individual goes out to fight [in accordance with the terms of this pact] or remains in his home, he will be safe unless he has committed a crime or is a sinner. [No one will be punished in his individual capacity for not having gone out to fight in accordance with the terms of this pact.]

57. Allah is the Protector of the good people and those who fear Allah, and Muhammad (may Allah bless him and grant him peace) is the Messenger of Allah. [He guarantees protection for those who are good and fear Allah.]

HESHAM A. HASSABALLA is a pulmonary/critical care physician currently practicing in the Chicago area. He is a columnist for Beliefnet.com, the premier religion and spirituality website. In addition to writing, he helped found the Chicago chapter of the Council of American-Islamic Relations, the nation's most prominent Islamic advocacy group, and he served on its executive board. He is also columnist for the Religion News Service, and his columns have been published in newspapers across the country. He lives with his wife and two daughters in the greater Chicago area.

KABIR HELMINSKI, an American Muslim, is a shaikh of the Mevlevi Order, which traces its lineage back to Rumi, the thirteenth-century Sufi mystic and poet. Helminski is the translator of many books on Rumi, including *Jewels of Remembrance* and *The Pocket Rumi*, as well as several collections of Islamic writings. The founder and codirector of the Threshold Society (Sufism.org), an educational foundation within the Mevlevi tradition, he is the author of two books on spirituality, *Living Presence* and *The Knowing Heart*, which have been translated into eight languages. He is also currently codirector of an international education project developing new Islamic curricula (see TheBook.org).

Ambassador **AKBAR AHMED**, Ibn Khaldun Chair of Islamic Studies, American University in Washington, D.C., and former High Commissioner of Pakistan, has published numerous books, films, and documentaries. His books include *Postmodernism and Islam: Predicament and Promise, Resistance and Control in Pakistan, Islam Today: A Short Introduction to the Muslim World,* and *Islam Under Siege: Living Dangerously in a*

Post-Honor World, among others. *Discovering Islam: Making Sense of Muslim History and Society* was adapted into a six-part BBC TV series entitled *Living Islam*. His latest, *After Terror: Promoting the Dialogue of Civilizations*, was co-edited with Dr. Brian Forst.

BELIEFNET is the leading multifaith spirituality and religion website. Through its newsletters and online, Beliefnet reaches four million people daily. It is the winner of numerous prestigious awards, including the Webby for Best Spirituality Site and the Online News Association's top award for general excellence for independent websites. Its book *Taking Back Islam* won the Wilbur Award for Best Religion Book of 2003.